Answers
to
Frequently Asked Questions
on
Parenting

[Part 3]

Drs. Ekram and M. Rida Beshir

amana publications

First Edition
(1433 AH/2012 AC)

Copyright © 1433 AH/2012 AC
amana publications
10710 Tucker Street
Beltsville, MD 20705-2223 USA
Tel. 301.595.5777
Fax 301.595.5888
Email amana@igprinting.com
www.amana-publications.com

Library of Congress Cataloging-in-Publication Data

Beshir, Ekram.
  Answers to frequently asked questions on parenting / Ekram Beshir and
M. Rida Beshir.-1st ed.
      p. cm.
  Includes bibliographical references.
  ISBN 159008-036-X (alk. paper)
  1. Child rearing-Religious aspects-Islam. 2. Parenting-Religious
aspects-Islam. 3. Muslim youth-North America-Conduct of life. 1. Beshir,
Mohamed Rida. II. Title.

HQ769.3.B45.2005
297.5'77-dc22
                                                          2005022410

Acknowledgements

We would like to express our sincere gratitude to our daughters, Noha and Sumaiya, for all the time and hard work they put into editing this book. We will be forever indebted to them for their gracious support and dedication to this work. May Allah bless them, keep them on the Straight Path and reward them with *Jannah*.

We kindly request that every reader make *du'a* for them.

Introduction

As we indicated in the introduction of part one of this series, during workshops and convention sessions, we usually allocate time to answer questions from the audience. We try our best during this time to respond to the questions we receive in the most comprehensive way. However, with a hot topic like parenting, particularly in North America, there is never enough time to give detailed answers and at the same time respond to as many audience members' questions as possible. Over the years, we have noticed that certain questions come up repeatedly during our parenting workshops and lectures in various conferences/conventions on the subject of raising children in the North American society. Because of this, we feel that these questions represent crucial issues of concern occupying the minds of the great majority of parents, and as such, they deserve to be addressed in enough detail to help clarify these issues and provide Muslim parents with the proper advice supported by the Qur'an as well as the teachings of Prophet Muhammad *SAAW*.

This is why we decided to write this series of books to answer "Frequently Asked Questions about Raising Children in North America."

This is part three of the series. We apologize for the delay and for not making it available to the reader right after part two as we promised when we started the series. Due to both our health conditions as well as a very busy traveling schedule presenting our parenting workshops, we were unable to find the proper time to put into part three of the series for some time. We thank Allah *SWT* that He blessed our time and effort, and finally with His grace, that we are able to present the reader with this work.

Part one of the series covered a variety of topics and included categories covering questions related to correcting behaviour, environment, Islamic identity, schooling, celebrations, sex education, and miscellaneous questions.

Part two covered a variety of topics ranging from character building and personality development to the environment. It also addressed questions relating to young children, pre-teens, and teens.

In this work, part three, the main categories discussed are related to building character and developing personality, correcting behaviour, Qur'anic memorization and prayer training, schooling and environment, role modeling, conflict resolution and miscellaneous questions. We tried our best to respect this categorization; however, with subjects like these, there was some overlap.

It is important to note that all the questions in this series are real and were asked on one occasion or another by attendees of a workshop, an audience member at a conference/convention, or during our live dialogue on various websites such as www.masnet.org and www.islamonline.net.

We would also like to emphasize that our methodology in answering these questions will, as is always the case with our books, be from an Islamic perspective, drawing heavily on verses of the Qur'an, teachings of Prophet Muhammad *SAAW*, and events of his *Seerah*. We will also, *insha'a* Allah, draw on the practical experience we have *walhamdulilah* gained from countless parenting and counseling sessions during the last two decades and our knowledge of child psychology.

We realize that this is a huge responsibility and we sincerely pray to Allah SWT to help us provide the right answers to these questions as well as to make this series benefit as many Muslim families as possible in their quest to be the best Muslim parents for their children. We also ask Him to protect our Muslim families, our Muslim youth, our Muslim children and the whole Muslim *Ummah*.

Readers may kindly note that throughout the book, all the Quranic verses and sayings of Prophet Muhammad *SAAW* mentioned are the English translations of the meaning of the original text in Arabic. Though we have striven to use the most accurate English translations available, we remind the reader that any and all translations are: firstly, not the original words of Allah *SWT* or His prophet *SAAW*, and secondly, can never be as accurate as the original Arabic text.

Drs. Ekram & M. Rida Beshir

Contents

MISCELLANEOUS

BUILDING CHARACTER
AND
DEVELOPING PERSONALITY

How to promote critical thinking among our children when the child asks a lot of questions and we get bugged, irritated, and angry by the way they ask their question?

Answer   Promoting critical thinking in our children is a very important matter because it teaches them how to make the right choice between alternatives. Parents are not going to be around their kids all the time when they are faced with a problem so they can help them in making the right choice. As such it is crucial to help them on how to make the right decision themselves via teaching them critical thinking. This is particularly true in today's environment of our children living in the West considering the popular teens culture and peer pressure they are facing and subjected to.

To be able to teach our children critical thinking, first as parents we should have an accommodating attitude towards our children's questions. As a matter of fact, we should even encourage their questions and they should feel that we are welcoming all their questions. Our children should feel very comfortable approaching us with their questions. Sometimes, parents' attitude turns the children away and makes them hesitate in asking questions. In some cases, this attitude has been developed because of the impolite way some children use when asking the question. Being irritated and getting bugged with your children's questions to the extent that you create a barrier between your-self and your children is not the proper way out. The solution is to teach them how to ask the question properly and politely. It is essential that we parents keep this channel of communications open between ourselves and our children.

Teaching our children critical thinking requires the following:

• Training them on how to make choice between alternatives. This could start from very young age. For example, for a three years old child, rather than dressing her in a certain outfit when you are going out, put two different outfits on her bed and ask her which of them she would like to wear going out. Allow her to make the decision and respect her choice. 5 years old child, you can check with him how he wants to spend his weekend. Ask him if he wants to go for a picnic or he would rather spend the time visiting his friend. Again, allow him to choose and respect his choice.

• Consulting with them on family matters and teaching them the consequences of each decision we make. For example, if the family plans to move to new house in a different part of the city or even in another city. Nothing wrong with getting your 6 years old in getting involved on the discussion. It is important to talk about the advantages and disadvantages of the move, particularly the ones relevant to your child such as a bigger pool of friends because the community in the new location is bigger, and a nice developed youth center with many activities, etc.

• Allow your children to make their own decisions particularly in non critical matters. Even if they make the wrong decision let them live with this mistake. With non critical matters, the risk is not high and they will learn from their mistake.

• Also you can use certain games to promote critical thinking with your children. Here is an example of a game we used to play with our grand- children. They were four and five years old when we played this with them. This game could be played with children up to seven or eight years old depending on the child's maturity. Here is how it is played:

- To set the tone, one of the parents or grand-parents would ask the other a simple question in a chanting tone such as "Could a goat be the daughter of a horse? Is this possible? Is this possible?" The other parent would respond also in a chanting tone: "Of course not. Of course not."

- Then one of the parents would ask the children the same question in a chanting tone. The other parent would respond to the question together with the children.

- One of the parents would ask another question where the answer is a clear No, such as: "Could a boy be the daughter of a cow? Is it possible? Is it possible?" The other parent would answer together with the children: "Of course not. Of course not." Again, please try always to make it in a chanting tone.

- One of the parents would ask another question where the answer is a clear Yes, such as: "Could a boy be the son of a man? Is it possible? Is it possible?" The other parent would answer together with the children: "Of course yes. Of course yes." Again, please try always to make sure your response is in a chanting tone. Kids love chanting and singing.

- After the parents take turns asking a few different questions, they should ask the children to take turns and come up with their own questions. You will be surprised with the kind of questions they will come up with. Again, respond to their questions in a chanting and singing way to keep the fun going.

- Please note that you should take into consideration the age of the children playing the game. The older they are, the more difficult the questions should be. If you feel that they find it difficult to answer your questions, adjust the level of difficulty of the questions to make it easier for them. Don't forget, if you make the questions very difficult and they can't answer any of them, they will give up and may not be eager to continue playing the game.

You can also use stories to promote critical thinking among your children. For example, you can come up with a story where the mom in the story is asking her son or daughter to go out and buy certain items from the corner store. You can list the items, such as salt, milk and eggs, to be bought by the child in the story. Then you can add one other item to the list, such as a door key, that does not fit in this category and that would not usually be available in the corner store. Then you can ask your children the following question: "Do you think the boy in the story will find everything on the list at the corner store?" Some children may realize that an item such as a door key is not sold at the corner store. Others may not realize that there is a problem. For those children who do not realize that one of the items does not fall under the same category as the rest, you should try to lead them to the right answer by asking more questions. For example, you could ask: "Do you think the boy will find eggs at the corner store? Do you think the boy will find milk at the corner store?" And so on until they realize that door keys are a different category than food and probably won't be sold at the corner store.

In the many workshops I have attended for you, you have emphasized that it is very important to raise strong and confident children, which is an idea I fully agree with. The question is what we as parents can do to achieve this very important goal. Can you please shed some light on this subject and provide us with some practical tips to help us in achieving this objective? Thank you

Answer   This is a very important question and deserves to be answered in detail. In chapter four of our book, ***Muslim Teens: Today's Worry, Tomorrow's Hope,***[1] we discuss the answer to this exact question. As such, we feel it is much easier for the reader that we repeat most of the material covering this issue here again, rather than asking the reader to consult with our earlier book. We feel that unless we succeed in training our teens to have strong personalities and to be confident in themselves and their belief system, we may very well lose them to the whirlwind of popular western teen culture. It is very difficult for teens who don't believe strongly in their values to resist the temptation of following the crowd. A teen needs this strong personality and belief to be able to stand against the flow and say no to certain situations. The clash is eminent, it will happen, and when it happens she needs this confidence and strong personality.

A teen that is confident in his way of doing things will not be shaken if his peers do not agree with him about the way he talks or dresses. When he is invited to a mixed party where alcohol will be served, he needs to

---

[1] Drs Ekram and Mohamed Rida Beshir; ***Muslim Teens: Today's Worry, Tomorrow's Hope,*** amana publications, Beltsville, Maryland, USA, 2nd edition, third printing, 2007

say NO in an assertive and confident way. When she is asked to smoke a cigarette or to take drugs, she needs to say NO with pride and conviction. For the teen, saying no needs to be a source of pride and victory rather than a source of defeat and failure.

This is why it is very important for parents to use ways and means of *tarbiyah* that help Muslim teens to build a strong personality. Parents need to use methods that will ensure that their teen be confident in her ability to do the right thing all times, and make the correct decision when she is faced with a specific situation.

How can we raise strong confident teens?

To achieve this goal, there are things that parents should do and things that they should avoid.

Things that parents should do:

1. Help your teen to be close to Allah and know Him better: Knowing and believing in Allah can be a great source of confidence and support for the teen. This means that he believes that Allah's word is the truth and this life is very short compared to the hereafter, which is eternal. He believes that Allah's reward is so great that it is easy to sacrifice temporary joy in this short life. This beautiful reward of paradise will always be before his eyes and in his mind to the extent that it will provide him with the strength he needs to say no to the temptations he faces.

Parents should try to link the teen to His creator starting from a young age.[2] This is an ongoing process that should never stop.

---

[2] See chapter two of *Meeting the Challenge of Parenting in the West; an Islamic Perspective.* by the authors for various tips to achieve this goal. amana publications, Beltsville, MD, USA

It should continue through the teenage years using reminders, as indicated by the *hadeeth* of the prophet PBUH, narrated by Ibn Abbas may Allah be pleased with him, who said, "One day I was riding behind the prophet PBUH when he said: O' my dear son, I wish to instruct you with some words. Adhere to the orders of Allah and safeguard the commandments of Allah, He will protect you. Safeguard His rights, and he will be ever with you. When you beg, beg of Him alone; and when you stand in need of his assistance, supplicate Allah alone for help. Remember that if all people desire to benefit you, they will be unable to bestow anything upon you except that which Allah has preordained for you. And if all of them agree to do you harm, they will not be able to afflict you with anything except that which Allah has predestined against you. The pens have been lifted and put aside and the ink of the book of predestination has dried up.'"[3]

Reminders such as this one will help the teen feel that Allah is with her, constantly supporting her and watching over her. She will always try her best to do the right thing wherever she is. The intimate knowledge and love of Allah and following His orders is definitely the prime source of all support. During the migration of the prophet *SAAW* from Makkah to Madinah, after he made all the plans and arrangements humanly possible for his trip, he fully put his trust in Allah *SWT*. When the disbelievers came up to the opening of cave Thawr where the prophet *SAAW* was hiding with Abu Bakr, may Allah be pleased with him, Abu Bakr was very concerned about the prophet's safety,

---

[3] At-Termithy

but the prophet *SAAW* assured him that Allah would protect them. The prophet's knowledge and love of Allah as well as his complete obedience of Allah's orders provided him with tranquility, a great sense of self confidence, and a feeling of security even in the most difficult situations.

2. Another source of confidence for your teen would be to know the prophet *SAAW* and take him as a role model. Once your teen has done this, she will love him and feel honored to be his follower. She'll believe that whatever he tells her is the truth and that it's the best thing for her in this life and the hereafter. This belief can come from reading a comprehensive and authentic biography of the prophet *SAAW*.

It is the parents' job to help their teen find the right source of knowledge about the prophet's life and the lives of his companions. These biographies are the most important element in motivating your teen and making her learn about these wonderful heroes who sacrificed their lives for the sake of spreading the truth and making the word of Allah supreme. Examples of courage and bravery in the prophet *SAAW*'s life and the lives of his companions, may Allah be pleased with them all, are limitless and are all sources of confidence for your teen. Make sure your teen joins the right study circles and listens to scholars who motivate and explain Islam as a complete way of life, a mission, and a movement. Don't limit your teen's exposure to just memorizing Qur'an and *hadeeth* without understanding what she is memorizing and without explaining how these verses and *ahadeeth* fit into her everyday life.

3. The teen should feel that his parents love him, understand his needs, know that he is facing a lot of peer pressure, and care about his well being. Parents should try their best to help him face his problems by giving their support. They should make him feel like he can relate to them and they can relate to him by doing simple things like calling him by a nickname he likes and sharing jokes. They should speak to him in the most loving and compassionate way. They should be sensitive to his needs and try to satisfy them. They should make him feel that his presence is welcomed and that he is wanted at all times.

4. The teen should feel that she is valuable, capable, and skilled in various areas where she is similar to her mainstream North American peers. She can participate in several activities related to her age group. She can drive a car, work on a computer, play certain sports and so on. This will require hard work and effort on the parents' part in their teen's life to train her to acquire these skills. Of course, this has to start early in the child's life.

5. Parents have to make sure that the teen's lifestyle is an active one. They can help fill his life with useful, entertaining, and exciting activities. He shouldn't feel like it's boring and tedious just because it's different from the mainstream. Parents can get their teen involved in Muslim activities and have him attend regular study circles where he meets with Muslim friends of the same age group. They can memorize Qur'an together, and learn about the life of the prophet *SAAW* and his companions in an interesting and attractive way. He can attend the *Jama'ah* prayer in the Mosque with his father or, if the Mosque is not close by, they can pray *Jama'ah* as a family at home. He can play certain

types of sports and go out with his family or community members on organized hiking trips and nature outings. He can attend regular Islamic camps, conferences, retreats and conventions. In a nutshell, he can put his energy towards useful activities and no spare time is left unfilled. If it is not filled with good things, it can't be left empty, or it will be filled with bad things. As it was said, "If you don't occupy yourself with good things, it will make you busy with bad things."

6. The teen has to learn how to make decisions and decide what is good for her. After all, life is all about making the right choice and taking the right decision and the prophet *SAAW* said, "Be keen about what is good for you and seek help from Allah."[4] Parents have to provide this training to make the right choice within the family from an early age. For example, at the age of three, rather than dressing their daughter in a certain outfit when they are going out, parents should show the child two acceptable sets of clothes and ask her which one she would like to where going to the Mosque. When she grows a little older, at the age of six or seven, parents should give her the choice on how she wants to spend her spare time on the weekend. Rather than saying, "we will do this and that on the weekend," they can ask her which she would prefer: to go and visit another Muslim friend, or go on a picnic with the family. Starting from age nine and ten, they should consult with her on various family affairs and issues. They should make her part of the decision-making process rather than imposing things on her or simply informing her that the family has decided to do so and so. At age twelve,

---

[4] Muslim

they should start training her how to handle certain responsibilities such as letting her make up the family budget for the week, and so on.

When you train your child at various ages to make her own decisions, she will be able to make the right one, insha' Allah, when she becomes a teenager and is faced with choices. She won't just follow her peers blindly, rather, she will asses and evaluate situations, weigh the negatives and the positives and, insha' Allah, choose the right choice because she has been through the training and it isn't the first time she is making a choice. But if the family hasn't provided such training, the chances are that their teen may follow the crowd because she doesn't know how to choose and say NO. This is an important element in building a strong personality and a confident teen.

7. The parent should train the teen to be independent by giving him the skills needed to serve himself and survive in his environment rather than being dependent on his parents for everything. For example, give him some guidance in how to do it, and then allow him to shop for himself.

8. Parents should be supportive and empathize with their teen. Be accepting and understanding of her view rather than critical and ridiculing. Parents who can guide through discussion, listen attentively, and allow their teen to express her point of view freely without getting angry, no matter how wrong it might be from the parents' perspective, can help dramatically in boosting their teen's self esteem and self confidence.

9. Another way of building a strong personality for a teen and increasing his self-confidence is for parents to give reasons for what they ask of him rather than simply saying, "Case closed. Do as I say and don't ask questions." Your teen needs a parent who doesn't feel insulted whenever he asks you "Why?" but instead, uses the opportunity to explain, encourages him to ask more, trains him to ask in a polite, proper, and respectful way, and shows the wisdom behind orders and issues. This goes a long way in building a strong personality and self-confidence for your teen.

10. Empower your teen through making her feel good about herself. When she feels good about herself, she won't be over-sensitive as to how others view her behavior or think of her actions. She will be able to stand out from the mainstream and confidently say NO to things she shouldn't do. Of course, this process has to be done in a careful way to make sure that the teen is not boasting or becoming arrogant. You need her to be proud of whom she is and what she believes in without being arrogant and looking down on others.

11. Allow him to ask questions, no matter what the subject is and train him for in depth and critical thinking. The Qur'an encourages in depth thinking in every area of life. In *Surah Abasa* when the Qur'an talks about food, it says what could be translated as:

"Then, let man look at his food. We pour forth water in abundance. And We split the earth in clefts. And We cause therein the grain to grow, and grapes and clover plants, and olives and Date palms, and gardens dense with many trees, and fruits and herbage to be a provision and benefit for you and your cattle".[5] It is very clear that the Qur'an didn't just provide a simple answer to the question of food; it went into great detail to describe the food production cycle. This is to teach us in depth thinking and not to stop at the superficial level of things, but always look beyond the immediate and obvious answer. Also in *Surah Al-kahf*, we were told the story/parable of the two men. One of them was given two gardens and was very arrogant. During the dialogue between them we notice that his companion responds to his arrogant attitude in this way:

"His companion said to him during the talk with him, 'Do you disbelieve in Him Who created you out of dust, then out of *Nutfah* (mixed semen drops of male and female discharge), then fashioned you into a man?'".[6] This way, he is reminding him of his origin and bringing more in depth thinking into the discussion that may trigger a positive change in the other person's attitude.

Here are some examples of how to use this principle to help your teen build a strong and confident personality

1. When your teen comes to you with a question that may be related to Islam that he couldn't answer to one of his peers, rather than answering the question for him directly, a better way is to identify some references for him and ask him to research

---

[5] (Q 80, V24-32)

[6] (Q 18, V 37)

the answer. When he comes up with the answer, ask him about it and give constructive criticism. At the same time, provide some suggestions to make his answer more comprehensive and complete. A good way to think of a more complete answer is to use "what if" questions and try to respond to them.

2. Occasionally ask your teen to critique an article or a book she has just finished reading. Try to help her by providing a list of questions as guidelines to the critique process.

These are all ways to help your teen develop an analytical mind that questions and examines the things that are presented to him. He will not follow a trend just because it's the popular thing to do. Instead, he will see if this idea is sound, and has its own merits and basis. Doing this, *insha'Allah*, will help him to have a strong and confident personality.

12. Another very important thing that parents can do to help raise a strong and confident teen is to recognize the teen's need to belong and be accepted. Belonging and feeling accepted is a basic need for every human being. In the early stages of a child's life, this need is mainly satisfied through the immediate family. The common activities practiced by the family create and sustain a strong bond and feeling of attachment among all family members. This basic need to belong stays with the individual through all stages of life, the early school years, the adolescent years and even the adulthood years. This fact was very clear even in the life of the prophet *SAAW* and his companions. When they migrated from Makkah to Madinah, it was reported in many incidents that most of the companions felt

homesick for Makkah and some of them even wrote poetry expressing their feelings and how much they missed Makkah and their life there. This shows that they were so attached to the place and to the experience that they felt living in Makkah. It was reported that the prophet *SAAW* said, "By Allah, you are the most beloved land to me. It is only because your people have driven me away from you that I have left; otherwise I would have never left you."[7]

There is a lesson here for parents when they reflect on this fact. Parents should appreciate their children's pressing need to be accepted and to feel like they belong. It is of paramount importance to fulfill this need for their teens.

Following are some practical examples of how to ensure that this need is being fulfilled in your teen's life but that, at the same time, the basic principles of Islam are not being compromised:

1. Encourage your teen to watch sports competitions on TV in moderation, such as figure skating competitions, hockey games, Olympic events, etc. This will give her something clean to talk about the next day at school with her peers rather than completely feeling isolated from her schoolmates.

2. Allow your teen to participate in some useful extra curricular activities such as the computer club, the yearbook committee, etc.

---

[7] At-Termithy

3. Once in a while, allow your teen to be part of a committee that prepares for certain school activities such as field days, sports competitions, or the end of year graduation ceremony.

Doing the above will raise your teen's level of confidence because he will be able to participate in activities with other kids and relate to them. As a result, he will not feel isolated or inferior to his peers.

Things that parents should avoid:

1. **Being critical or pointing fingers.** The prophet *SAAW* taught us the etiquette and proper way of giving advice; It should be in private, not in public. If it has to be in public, we should not point fingers at the individual who made the mistake, rather the advice should be given in general terms, "Why are certain people doing/saying so and so?"[8]

This rule should be observed by parents when they deal with children's mistakes, especially if they have more than one child. It is very important not to accuse or chide your child, particularly in the presence of his friends or peers. This makes him more defensive. Talking in private is much more effective, as it gives the child the chance to think about the actual situation and not about the embarrassment he is feeling. The disadvantages of criticizing in public certainly outweigh the advantages. It is humiliating and embarrassing for your teen and it will certainly not help him to have a strong and confident personality. But if we follow the advice of the prophet *SAAW*, insha' Allah we can

---

[8] Muslim

help our teen to achieve the strong confident personality we all want for him.

2. **Perfectionism**. It was reported that Prophet Muhammad *SAAW* has said, "The hasty one, neither covers the desired distance, nor spares the back of his means of transportation."[9] The "hasty one" was explained by the scholars as the one who lost the companionship of his fellow travelers because he caused the beast he was riding to be fatigued. The perfectionist is similar to the hasty one; he or she asks others to do more than they can bear, and in the process he causes them to be fatigued and think that they are good for nothing because of his continuous criticism of what they do. This is not healthy behavior, especially with children because it lowers their self esteem.

3. **Over protection**. No doubt protecting children is one of the very important duties of parents. However, parents should be aware of the very fine line between protection and discouragement. Over protecting may give the impression to our children that we as parents think they are incapable. This for sure will lead to lower self esteem and will not help us in our quest to raise strong confident children

4. **Humiliation**. When Allah *SWT* instructs us in Qur'an not to call each others names or humiliate one another[10], this applies to everyone, including parents and children. A child who is

---

[9] Albazzar

[10] See Q 49, V 11

humiliated by his parents will certainly have a very weak personality.

For more practical examples on the above to avoid components, please consult chapter one of our book "Parenting in the West"[11]

The above to do list and to avoid list, if followed properly, will insha'a Allah go long way in making sure that your teen will be strong, confident, and proud of her identity.

---

[11] *Meeting the Challenge of Parenting in the West: An Islamic Perspective* by Drs. Ekram and Mohamed Rida Beshir, fourth edition, amana publications Beltsville, MD, USA, 2007

I have three children, two boys who are 9 and 7, and a girl who is 6 years old. We try to raise them according to Islamic principles as best as we can. We know that it is important for them to mix with friends other than their siblings, so we try our best to visit other families who have children around the same age. The problem is that some of those families don't meet our Islamic standards. What should we do? Is it better not to spend time with those friends, so they are not affected by their bad traits? Or is it better to allow them to mix and visit with those kinds of children and live with the consequences?

Answer   This is a very good question and it is important to discuss since it's something many Muslim families face. Our advice for the questioner is to consider the following points:

• Children need to mix with friends. They learn many things and acquire various social skills from these visits, such as how to interact with others, how to take turns, etc. As such, the wider the group they mix with, the better.

• Of course, friends affect each other's behavior and have a great influence on each other. This is emphasized in many of the sayings of Prophet Muhammad *SAAW*. As such, it is important to teach our children how to select and choose their friends. It is important to help them find the friends who can have a positive and healthy impact on their personality, and avoid those who would have a negative influence on their moral and ethical behaviour. This help could come in the form of teaching them the right criteria of friend selection, as well as hosting friends at your home, or driving your children over to visit their friends, even when they don't live close by. Yes, it may be inconvenient, but it is important to lend whatever help we can to our children in this area.

• The above can usually be easily done in large cities where the size of the Muslim community is considerable. We realize that in North America, particularly in the cases of small Muslim communities, this is usually easier said than done. Because of this, some families may have no option but to allow their children to mix with other children who may not fully adhere to Islamic rules as their own children do. Here is what we recommend for those families:

- Do your homework and get to know the family of the children that you want your child to mix with. You may need more than one visit. The better you know the family, the better a decision you can make for whether your child can mix with them regularly.

- Start first by hosting the other children at your home for the first few visits, so you can have better supervision and control of what happens during the visit.

- Don't invite large a number of children at once. Try to limit the invited number to two or three friends at the most.

- Prepare your child for the visit. Talk to him about the manners and etiquettes of hosting friends at our homes and how to be good to them, as well as making sure that whatever we do during the visit will not displease Allah *SWT*

- At the beginning of the visit, give very clear instructions to every one laying down your expectations and promise certain rewards if they adhere and follow your rules until the end of the visit. Follow up on your promises at the end of the visit.

- During the visit, make sure you deal with any issue that may arise in the proper way. Make sure you don't tolerate bad behavior

- After each visit, monitor the change in your child's behaviour. Evaluate the positive and the negative impact on your child. If you notice some changes you don't like, talk to your child about them and let her know that these visits with those friends may be suspended if the same behavior persists.

• As parents we should also consider the other side of the coin. Many parents try to find friends who have an equal or higher level of Islamic commitment as their children to befriend. Therefore, sometimes we should also try to help children who may not be fully adhering to Islamic principles and may have certain minor behavioural shortcomings by letting our more committed children befriend them. In cases like this, a few precautions should be taken into consideration:

- Make sure that the behavioural problems exhibited by those other children are not major and can be corrected with a little bit of work and good companionship

- Talk to your child and let him know that it is part of our duties as Muslims to help others who may need our help. This help is not only in the physical sense but it also includes supporting others to do the right thing. As such he has a duty to help other children to correct their mistakes. By having this conversation, you are setting your child up to have a positive effect over the other children and to earn a reward for doing this.

- Remind the child to have the proper intention while she is doing this so she can be rewarded for her actions. Also remind her to be humble and never to look down at other children who may not know as much as she knows about their *deen*. Remind her to thank Allah *SWT* for His guidance to her.

- Monitor the situation after each interaction with the other children. Find out if there are any negative changes in your child's behaviour. Reassess, evaluate the situation and make changes as necessary. On the other hand, if you notice any positive changes with the other children, no matter how little they may be, thank your child and remind him of the great reward he will get from Allah *SWT*. In some cases, you may also like to reward him yourself with something tangible. Also use every opportunity to encourage your child to continue doing the good work he is doing.

My daughter is 7 year old. She is a good child who tries to do her best. Sometimes she wants to do something that may be too hard for her. She says, "In the name of Allah most Compassionate, most Merciful" and expects that this thing will be done. Other times she wishes for things to happen that she wants badly, and makes Dua'a for them to happen. When things don't happen as she expects, she feels let down and asks, 'How come Allah didn't listen to my Dua'a?' I don't know how to answer her when she asks these kinds of questions.

Answer   This question provides a golden opportunity for parents to instill certain Islamic concepts in the heart and mind of their daughter. Following are some of these concepts:

• Allah created universal laws to govern everything in our life and in the whole universe, particularly, the law of cause and effect. An important part of cause and effect is that our actions have consequences. For anything to happen, a person would have to work towards making it happen. For example, if a student wants to have good grades, he has to study seriously and do his homework. Give your daughter an example that she can relate to easily, such as something as simple as the family's breakfast. In the morning, when your family sits down for breakfast, the food doesn't just appear for them to eat. Mom, dad, or one of the older siblings has to take the eggs out of the fridge, prepare it for the rest of the family, and put it on the table so everyone can eat. Likewise, we have to work for everything else. If we want certain things to happen we have to take the necessary actions and steps so they can happen *insha'a* Allah.

• The concept of *dua'a* is another important concept to teach our children. *Dua'a* is a form of worship that brings us closer to Allah *SWT*. At the same time, it is a tool and privilege that Allah *SWT* gave to us to use when we need to seek His help. However, there are manners and etiquettes to be followed when we make *dua'a*. Here are a few of them:

- With the *dua'a*, we also have to work hard and exhaust our means to try to reach the results and achieve the goals we are aspiring towards.[12]

- It is recommended to make *dua'a* while you are in a state of purity. If you can perform ablution before you make *du'a*, this is good because it is an act of worship and you should try your best to get rewarded the most for it.

- You do your best and should be content with whatever results are achieved. Accept Allah's decision for you and be sure that it will be the best in the long term *insha'a* Allah, even if it seems different from what you were looking for or trying to achieve

---

[12] (Q27, V62)

• Teach your daughter that Allah *SWT* responds to our *dua'a* in different ways, such as the following:

    - Granting the person her wish directly.

    - Not granting the wish directly, but saving it for the person and granting him something better later in his life or in the Hereafter.

    - Not granting the wish directly, but preventing something bad that was going to happen to the person from happening.

In all of the above cases, whatever response we get will be the best for us because Allah *SWT* knows everything. Human knowledge can not encompass all factors of a situation, so a person may want something and make *dua'a* for it, while it's not actually the best for thing for her.

Q. 5

My daughter is 14 years old and my son is 12 years old. Alhamdulellah they are doing OK academically at school. Throughout their childhood, I've tried to keep them at home away from any risk of danger. I haven't allowed them to take part in any extra-curricular activities for fear of the culture they'd be exposed to, and the things they might learn there that I don't want them to know about. The problem is that they always complain that they're bored, and they are not very welcoming to the idea of just memorizing more Qur'an as a way to fill their time. They are always asking to watch TV and sit long hours in front of the computer. Whenever I object to this, they say 'there is nothing else for us to do'

Answer   There are many important parenting issues raised in the question that deserve to be discussed in details: The issue of not allowing the children to participate in any extra-curricular activities, the issue of spending long stretches of time in front of the TV and computer, *Qura'nic* memorization, the importance of utilizing our time properly and not wasting it just to name a few. Let us now discuss these issues one by one.

• Not allowing our children to be part of any extra-curricular activities may not be the best way to protect them from unwanted negative cultural effects. Not only this, but it will also deprive them from satisfying one of their basic needs, which is the need to belong. Certain extra-curricular activities could be good for them to satisfy this need. We should not classify all these activities as bad or unacceptable to us as Muslims, rather, we should consider that some of them are useful and have a positive impact on our children's personality. Muslim parents should do their homework and find out which extra-curricular activities don't contradict our values, and allow their children to be part of some of these activities. At the same time, we should help our children to resist the negative effects of the culture by making them proud of their identity as Muslims and confident of whom they are. Strengthening their belief, loving and accepting them for whom they are, helping them to be capable and highly skilled, and teaching them critical thinking are some of the ways to make them confident and proud of their identity.[13]

• Your children's complaints that they're bored is a natural consequence of their not being provided with an active lifestyle. Parents should get their children involved in different activities, and provide them with the opportunity to be active at home, with community projects, and with certain mainstream activities. At home, they should be part of planning various family projects, carrying out certain chores, and participating in family activities. Parents should also facilitate for their children to be part of Muslim community youth groups and get them involved in as many community projects as they can. At the mainstream level, we can help our children take part in certain volunteer activities such as volunteering in hospitals, public libraries,

---

[13] See "Have a vision" section of the authors DVD "Positive Parenting Skills Based on Qur'an and Sunnah" by Mosaic production for in-depth analysis of how to make our children confident and proud of their identity. See also the answer of question 2 in this book

fundraising for good causes like the cancer society, etc.

• Research indicates that excessive TV watching has many negative effects on various areas of our life. Among these areas are the following:

- Reading ability,
- IQ, imagination,
- Language patterns,
- Critical thinking,
- Hyperactivity,
- Self image

In addition, the amount of violence on TV is increasing tremendously year by year, and it has very devastating effects on our children, particularly boys. Direct copying, disinhibition of aggressive and antisocial behaviour, value-shaping and cultivating effect, and diverting attention from more important matters are some of the specific effects of TV violence.[14]

Because of all of the above, we don't recommend that children spend a lot of time in front of the TV. Providing them with an active lifestyle as a positive alternative will no doubt help in reducing their TV watching time.

• This situation provides parents with a golden opportunity to discuss with their children the concept of time in the life of a

---

[14] See chapter 3 of our book *Meeting the Challenge of Parenting in the West; An Islamic Perspective* published by amana publications

Muslim and the importance of utilizing it properly. Here are some significant points that parents can use in this discussion:

- Importance of time in Qur'an
- Allah makes an oath and swears by time in many of the chapters of the last *juz'* of Qur'an such as:
- By the night when it conceals and covers. And by the day when it appears[15]
- By the dawn and by the ten nights[16]
- By the morning brightness and by the night when it covers with darkness[17]
- By time[18]

• Many verses instruct Muslims to take lessons from the alternation of day and night[19]

- Importance of time in Sunnah (the life of the Prophet)
- Two among the four questions that everyone will be asked on the Day of Judgment before he or she can move are related to time. These are questions about our life in general and the years of our youth in particular

• All acts of worship are related to time in one way or the other

---

[15] (Q 92, V 1,2)
[16] (Q 89, V 1,2)
[17] (Q 93, V 1,2)
[8] (Q 103, V 1)
[19] For example, see Q 24, V 44. See also Q 25, V 62

- *Salat* is at a prescribed time[20]
- *Zakat* is also related to time because it has to be paid annually after the *nisab* is reached. *Nisab* is the amount one's net worth must exceed for the Muslim owner to be obligated to give *zakat*.
-Fasting is also to be observed in a specific month of the lunar calendar (Ramadan)[21]. It also has to be done between the times of dawn and sunset.[22]
-Hajj also has to be performed at a specific time in the lunar calendar [23]
• The advice in the tablets of Prophet Ibraheem *SAAW* told us to organize our time properly and divide it into various balanced portions to cover our spiritual, emotional, social, and physical needs.[24]

There is no doubt that *Qur'anic* memorization is wonderful and very noble cause, and we should encourage our children to memorize as much Qur'an as possible. However, it will be more interesting and beneficial if they study the explanation of what they memorize even if this is going to reduce the quantity they memorize. Certain chapters of Qur'an will provide them with many important concepts they need at this age and will make them stronger Muslims *insha'a* Allah.

---

[20] (Q 4, V 103)

[21] (Q 2, V 185)

[22] (Q 2, V 187)

[23] (Q 2, V 197)

[24] Ibn Heban

CORRECTING BEHAVIOR

Q. 6

I need some suggestions on how to deal with a stubborn child who is about 5 years old. I have been having problems with my son and have tried many different ways to solve them, without success. Basically, he is extremely stubborn. At school, he has been hitting other kids a lot, and though I discuss this with him and warn him that it's not acceptable behavior, he continues to do it. More than once at home, he has damaged household items or made huge messes. When he asks for something, he expects to get it right away and gets quite upset if he doesn't. Once, I gave him paper to color on, but he refused to color on it and started to color elsewhere. I have tried many different ways to change his behavior, such as giving him time outs, taking away his toys or forbidding him from doing things he likes, and not allowing him TV time. I repeatedly tell him 'No' when he misbehaves, and I sometimes get angry and shout at him, but nothing seems to help. He has two older siblings, a boy who is 19 years old, and a girl who is 18 years old. I hope you can help me with this problem.

Answer   It seems as though there is a lack of consistency and structure in your child's life. Apparently, the many 'No's' you have been saying to him are being said in the heat of the moment, and as such, they are not effective. Also, since he is the baby of the family with two older siblings who are almost 15 years older than him, we sense that he must have been pampered and spoiled a bit by the adults in his life. The solution to his problem would involve bringing consistency and structure into his life, combined with affection from both parents, as well as using effective methods of discipline. As such, to correct his situation we suggest the following:

1. Please stop labeling your child as "stubborn". We are instructed by Qur'an in *Surah Al Hujjorat* to avoid calling each others names[25]. When you label the child with a certain quality or call him a certain name, this is the impression and the image he will have of himself. He will try to fulfill your description of him. Children see themselves in their parents' mirror and become what the parents attribute them to be. They fulfill the parents' prophesy.

2. Please set clear and firm limits for your son in various areas of his life. From your description of the problem, it seems that he doesn't know his limits or that he was never made aware of these limits in a clear way, and so he continues to whine and expect more. Since he has been used to not having limits for sometime, this is going to be new for him and he will likely resist observing these limits. As such, this limit-setting should be combined with affection. Be gentle and kind, and show genuine affection when introducing this new element to his life.

3. Practice proper and effective discipline. Reinforcement is a

---

[25] (Q49, V11)

very important and successful method of discipline. Guiding your son's behaviour to the right path through reinforcement is a very appropriate technique. When your son has obeyed you and has done something positive, reward him by introducing something positive in his environment; for example, taking him for an outing to his favorite park, eatery or store. But when your son has done something negative, you punish him by withdrawing what he likes the most; for example, withdrawing a favorite dish or not allowing him to watch his preferred TV cartoon. Another very important point in proper discipline is seriousness. When correcting your child you should be serious. Laughing or giggling and not being serious will not get you anywhere.

4. Be consistent in applying the discipline. Be firm; for example, if you have refused to allow your child view television late at night, stick to it. The child may cry, weep and wail, and may also make a huge scene, but don't give in. Once you give in, the child will know how to get his way every time he wants something.

5. Be wise in picking your fights with your child. Parents should learn to pick their battles carefully. For many smaller issues, they can allow their children to make their own decisions, such as which outfit to wear, or whether the family should have peas or carrots with chicken for dinner. For other issues, you need to be completely inflexible. For example, no amount of arguing should let your stubborn child get out of wearing his seat belt in the car. You need to learn how you can properly engage your child and respond to behavior that you want to minimize or eliminate.

6. Use modeling. It is a known fact among all *Tarbiyah* scholars that modeling or leading by example is the most effective tool of parenting. Please look at yourself or the main adults in the life of your child and ask these questions: are you or your husband stubborn? Do either or both of you display this trait often at home? If yes, your son may be imitating your behaviour and acting the same way that you are behaving. As such, if you want to change your son, make an attempt to change yourself first. A combination of stubborn child and stubborn parent may lead to a lot of tension.

7. When correcting your son, don't be harsh, and try to control your anger. Be firm and assertive, but under no condition should you lose control and start shouting and yelling at your son. If he doesn't obey your instructions, simply repeat them again in an assertive and calm voice, but neither give up to his demands nor lose your temper and become angry. As soon as your son detects anger in your voice, he will respond the same way and continue to demonstrate negative behaviour.

We also encourage you to look on the positive side. What you may consider stubbornness may just be a combination of persistence and willfulness. These are traits of leadership that, if handled properly when your child is young, will help your child to grow to be a very effective and leading member of the *Ummah*, not just a follower. As such, stubbornness can mean that your child is spirited, sure of himself, and probably demonstrates a lot of stick-to-itiveness. Try the above suggestions even if it may be difficult for you, so we can have a good Muslim leader in the near future *insha'a* Allah. It is worth the effort, and the reward from Allah is so beautiful.

If this doesn't work and he continues to displays this irritable behavior constantly out side home, this requires a professional evaluation most probably by a pediatric mental health professional. It is important to find out if there is any family history of mood disorder or other type of emotional condition. The mental health professional should also look at the possibility of any major changes or transitions in the life of your child in particular and in your family in general that may be contributing to this problem.

How can I help my angry child? I have 5 year-old boy who seems to always be angry for one reason or another. I'm not sure what is causing all of anger, or what the reason for it could be. Can you please suggest some tips on how to deal with this situation? I really appreciate your help. Thank you

Answer   To start with, let us agree that anger is a natural emotion and is created by Allah for certain reasons. As such, no person or family can be anger-proof. However, there are ways you can help your child get a handle on anger. Here are some suggestions for you to consider:

• **Inner peace**.

There is no doubt that a person who is connected to Allah *SWT* is usually calmer, and feels more peaceful and content. As such, in *Surah Al-ra'd*, Allah reminds us to remember Him so our hearts will be in a state of comfort and serenity[26]. Research has shown, and our experience supports this observation, that parents and children who are connected to Allah, get angry with each other less often. As such, we recommend that parents invest in the spiritual development of their children and should link them to their creator to help them achieve inner peace[27]. The connected child, growing up with a sense of well- being, will still get angry, but he or she learns to handle the anger in

---

[26] (Q13, V 28)

[27] See Chapter two of our book *Meeting the Challenge of Parenting in the West; An Islamic Perspective* on tips on how to link your child with the Creator

such a way that it does not take over his or her personality. Parents who are connected and have inner peace will invest time into getting to know their children well, so they are less likely to create situations that provoke them and their children to anger. Attached parents know they don't have to be harsh to be in control.

The unconnected child operates from inner turmoil. He has no inner peace. Down deep this child feels something important is missing in himself and he is angry about it. (This feeling may continue into adulthood.) This void is likely to reveal itself as anger toward himself and parents, placing everyone at risk of developing feelings of anger.

• Help your child not to accumulate anger

As parents, try your best to be attentive listeners. This way you will be able to help your child work through his or her feelings. When you show empathy rather than judgment and willingly listen to your children, they will often talk themselves out of their fit of temper. This way, you are encouraging your child to recognize when he or she is angry, even for children as young as toddlers. To illustrate this concept, here is a real life example that happened with Aisha, a seven years old daughter of a friend we have been counselling. Aisha was insisting on watching a certain TV program. Her mom disagreed, and she became angry. She felt that she absolutely had to watch the program. Her mom felt that the program content was harmful to her growing self and to family harmony. The mom listened attentively and non-judgmentally while Aisha pled her case. After she had made her appeal, the mom made hers. With calm authority, the mom made her own points, while conveying to Aisha that she understood but did not agree with her viewpoint. The mom intelligently asked Aisha probing questions, such as: "What about the program is so important to you?" "Do you understand why I don't want you to watch it?" "Could you think of an activity that is more fun than watching this program?" "Are you just bored? If so, I have an idea..." Gradually Aisha realized that this program was not worth getting so worked up about. As the dialogue continued, her eyes dried and her reddened face relaxed. The mom ended this encounter with a chuckle about how Aisha had let such a stupid program upset her. Aisha's mom also went outside to skip rope with her daughter instead.

• Model

In counseling parents of angry children, we have found two main causes for their anger: Sometimes, there is a lot of family anger – the mother and/or father is on edge all the time and the child incorporates these feelings as part of herself; the other main cause is that the child feels angry because her sense of well-being is threatened. Helping angry children to control their anger starts with the proper modelling from the parents. Parents have to learn how to control their anger and if for any reason they have to express it, they should learn how to express it properly. The Prophet Muhammad *SAAW* gave us lots of advice on controlling our anger[28]. Not only this, but he, *SAAW*, also prescribed several methods for managing it[29]. Parents should

---

[28] See chapter 2 of our book *Meeting the Challenge of Parenting in the West: An Islamic Perspective* published by amana- publications

[29] See chapter 2 of our book *Meeting the Challenge of Parenting in the West; an Islamic Perspective* published by amana- publications

learn these techniques and model them for their children to help reduce and control their anger.

Modelling how to express anger also helps in having a less angry child. Anger that is expressed inappropriately blocks your ability to discipline wisely and puts a barrier between you and your child. Displays of anger scare children and put them on the defensive. They will either retreat into a protective shell or grow to have an angry personality themselves. Small children are devastated by the sight of big, scary, out-of-control daddy or raging mommy. They fear that the parent will stop loving them, hurt them, or leave. You don't want your child to have to squelch the flow of his normal feelings because he's frightened of what he might set off in you. Staying calm in the face of any feeling (anger, fear, even love) is a measure of emotional maturity. Your child will learn how to handle his anger by watching you. Communicating your expectations to the child before hand of what makes you angry will also help reduce angry situations.

• Emphasize the child's positive actions

Try to think about some of the good traits that your angry child possesses. Praise these traits and talk about them in a positive tone. Don't dwell on the bad behaviour of your angry child. It's devastating for a child to feel that she is a "bad kid." Unless that feeling is reversed, the child grows up acting the part. To get the "bad" feeling out of your child, intervene with a reassuring "You're not bad, you're just young, and young people sometimes do foolish things. But Daddy is going to help you stop doing these things so you will grow up feeling like you are the nice person I know you are." This sends a message to your child that you care enough to find the good child beneath the bad behavior. Also remember, Sister, that no one is perfect. The prophet *SAAW* has said: "All sons of Adam make mistakes, and the best of those who makes errors are those who try to repent and correct their mistakes.[30]"

Mistakes are a good way to learn. Try to do a lot of learning in your family. When one of you makes a mistake, try to comment: "Now, what can we learn from this situation?" If the anger button gets pushed this won't work. Be careful not to react in an angry way when someone spills his milk or tears his pants. Just say, "Now what can we learn from this?" Then, maybe even have a laugh over it.

---

[30] Ahmad, Ibn Majjah and others

I'm having a big problem with some of my children. I think they lie to me in many instances, and I don't know why. I know that lying is a very bad quality, and that Muslims shouldn't lie. I would like to raise my children as honest and trustworthy Muslims. I don't want them to lie to me or to anyone else, for that matter. Do you have any advice for me? I really appreciate your help in this matter. Thank you

Answer   Telling the truth and being honest is a universal value recognized by all religious as well non religious communities. Islam emphasizes this important fact in many verses of the Qur'an in various ways. In some verses Allah praises those who are truthful.[31] In other verses He says that on the Day of Judgment, truthfulness will benefit those who practiced it in this life and that they will be rewarded with Paradise.[32] The sayings of Prophet Muhammad *SAAW* are also full of great advice relating to this important subject, such as the fact that truthfulness will lead to paradise and telling lies will lead to hellfire.[33]

I wish the questioner was more specific. It would have helped us tremendously in answering the question if we knew the age of the child who is lying, how many children there are, their various age, and a little information on the family dynamics. This would have been greatly

---

[31] (Q19, V54)

[32] (Q5, V119)

[33] See the book of **Riad-ul Saleheen**, chapter four (Truthfulness) for many saying of Prophet Muhammad on the subject

helpful in providing a more specific and precise answer to the question. I think the best we can do for a question like this is to provide some general guidelines and hope it will help *insha'a* Allah.

Young children between 3-5 years old are full of curiosity and imagination. Their imagination is very vivid to them. They are not sure where the real ends and the unreal begins. This could be one of the reasons they love stories. Also, because of this they can make up imaginary stories occasionally. Some parents confuse this with lying, but it is not for this age group. It is part of the way they express their imaginations. Parents shouldn't be alarmed about this unless it becomes excessive. As a matter of fact, a little imagination and expressing this imagination is a good thing. When this becomes too much, the reason may be that the child is left alone for long periods of time without engaging in activity with other children. The remedy is simple in such cases, mainly, to do the following two things:

> 1. Find other children in the same age group and provide the child with the opportunity to play and spend time with those children

> 2. Ask yourself as a parent if your child is spending enough "relaxed" time with you. If not, please make sure you provide him with a lot of this kind of companionship, including hugging, gentle play-wrestling, and piggyback rides. The Prophet *SAAW* use to carry Al-Hassan and Al Hussain, his grandsons, on his back and act like a camel for them and he uses to tell them, "the best camel is yours and the best riders are you."[34]

---

[34] Muslim

The above two suggestions are enough to help reduce excessive imagination by children.

As for older children, when they lie, we should ask ourselves why they do this. The key to solving their lying is to find the reason for why they are doing it in the first place. Everyone, adult or child, gets into a jam occasionally when the only tactful way out is a small lie. Psychologists say that this is not a cause for alarm unless it becomes a pattern.

Knowing the motive no doubt would help parents to find a solution for their children's lying. Here are some of the reasons that cause older children to resort to lying:

• **Avoiding punishment;** imagine a scenario where the mother discovers that something is missing from the house, and tries to find out who took that specific item. As soon as one of the children confesses that it is he who took the item, she punishes him. Next time, this child may resort to lying and deny having anything to do with the incident to avoid his mom's punishment. Another example is that, whenever a child brings her report card home, her father scolds her for any grade that may have not met his expectation and never comments on the good grades. This child may try not to tell her parents about her report card. When she is asked, she may lie and say it is not out in an effort to avoid punishment. Instead of scolding the child, parents must try to find out why their child wasn't able to get a good grade in certain subjects. Is it because she is not paying attention during the class? Is it because the teacher is not explaining the subject properly? Or is it because the child is distracted and not focused during her study at home? When the reason is known, the suitable help can be provided for the child and lying can be avoided.

• **Wrong model**; Children may lie because we as parents are committing the same mistake. For example, a father tells his daughter, who is answering the phone to tell the caller that he (the father) is not home. Modeling is the most important tool there is in parenting. Parents should try their best to model the good character they want to instill in their child in order for the child to pick it up.

• **Feeling neglected at home;** Parents' attention and approval is a basic need for children. As such, when parents neglect providing enough attention to their children while they are behaving properly, children may resort to lying to attract their parents' attention.

• **Lack of fulfilling emotional needs**; not satisfying the emotional needs of children can leave negative marks on the child's personality. Among these negative marks can be lying.

• **Parents not fulfilling their promises to children**; many parents make lots of promises to their children without thinking about them or having the intention to honor such promises. When this is done repeatedly, children lose trust in these promises and in almost everything parents tell them to do. They try to escape from carrying out any of the parents' orders and this can lead them to lie to their parents.

• **Bad company;** many children spend lots of time outside home. If their friends lie, they may pick up the same bad habit. The Prophet *SAAW* warned us of befriending those who may have a negative effect on us.[35] As such, it is important that we teach our children the proper criteria for selecting friends, as well as help in seeing those good friends by driving our children to their houses to visit, or hosting those friends in our home.

• **The love of being popular and in the spotlight;** many children want to belong to the popular group at the school. One way of doing this is to posses things to show that they are worthy of being part of the popular group. Another way is to give the already "popular kids" gifts in order to be accepted. When parents of those children don't buy them what they ask for, they (the children) may resort to lying to get these things.

---

[35] Ahmad and Al-Bayhaqy

I have four children. The first two are 15 and 14 years old. The second are 6 and 7 years old. They are all boys. The older two boys have been fighting with each other since they were very young. I can't remember exactly when they started fighting, maybe as early as when they were 5 and 4 years old. No matter what I did, they would get along for extremely brief periods, then start fighting again for the most trivial reasons. Recently I noticed that the two youngest boys have also started fighting with each other for any and everything. What is happening with my children? Our home is not bearable any more. Is this sibling rivalry? How can I stop their fighting and get them to love and care for each other? Please help. Thank you in advance.

Answer   To answer this question, it is important for parents to understand the underlying reasons for sibling rivalry. The more parents know about the reasons, the better they are equipped to be able to reduce it in their family. Here are the main reasons for sibling rivalry:

• Lack of fairness from the parents' side. This means that one or both parents favor one or more of their children over the others

• Comparing siblings. This creates a negative atmosphere in the family and almost always leads to sibling rivalry.

• Inconsistency or even perceived inconsistency on the parents' side in their dealings with the children, either when they make the same mistake, or even when they have a similar achievement.

Here are some guidelines to help this family reduce sibling rivalry among their children:

• As usual, modeling comes at the top of these guidelines. When parents avoid arguing in front of their children and exhibit cooperation in all their dealings, there is no doubt that this will help children to follow suit and will reduce sibling rivalry in the family. Check your behavior as a parent and be honest with yourself. Try to find out if you argue a lot, or if you lose your temper in front of the children. If this is the case, you must make a serious effort to stop this kind of behavior, especially in front of your children.

• Stay positive. Rather than using a blaming attitude and pointing fingers or labelling one of the children as the trouble maker, try to use any conflicts or incidents that arise to teach your children valuable lessons. Take an attitude of asking, "What can we learn from this." It's very healthy and results in a warm and comfortable family atmosphere.

• Begin the day in harmony. When we start our day with the early morning prayer (*Fajr Salat*) then follow it up with the morning supplications (*Azkar Al Sabah*) as recommended to us by Prophet Muhammad *SAAW*, it puts blessing (*Barakah*) in our day and creates an atmosphere of harmony within the family. It is recommended that we do the prayer together in *Jamaa'h* as a family and also do the morning supplications together as a group. Make one of the children lead the supplications and the rest of the family repeat after her. Remember to rotate leading the supplication among the children. Having the same child leading the supplications every day will defeat the purpose and send the wrong message to the other children.

• Hold family meetings to discuss various issues, and use them to talk about cooperation and sharing. Try to make each child come up with stories from the life of Prophet Muhammad *SAAW* and his companions illustrating how they helped each other and cooperated in various matters. It is important to teach our children to take after the Prophet Muhammad *SAAW* and the *Sahabah* as role models in various aspects of our life. Also in these meetings, try to come up with some ground rules regarding the way you deal with conflicts in general and sibling rivalry in particular. Involve your children in setting these ground rules. They are much more likely to adhere to rules if they were part of setting them in the first place.

• Set limits that everyone in the family must respect. Make these red flag limits part of the above agreed upon rules.

• Listen—really listen—to how your children feel about what's going on in the family.

• Be there for each child. Set aside "alone time" for each child and make sure each child has enough time and space of their own.

• Plan family activities that are fun for everyone such as picnics, sports where all family members can participate, bowling or curling, etc.

• Teach your kids positive ways to get attention from each other, such as proposing an interesting game to the other sibling, sharing a book or a toy for the younger siblings, or watching an interesting DVD together, etc.

• Set your kids up to cooperate rather than compete. You can do this by rewarding all actions of cooperation.

• Don't compare siblings to each other; rather, try to compare the progress of each child separately. For example, use opportunities such as the month of Ramadan or two Eids to compare a child's progress in various areas, such as the amount of Qur'an learned.

• Sometimes, it's best not to intervene, particularly in minor situations. Let your children try to find solutions for their own quarrels on their own. This will go a long way in training them in conflict resolution, and will help them develop the skills to work out their conflicts on their own.

• Use times of calm to teach conflict resolution, when the atmosphere is conducive to cooperation. Trying to teach conflict resolution in the heat of the moment does not work, as each child becomes defensive and refuses to cooperate.

• Don't yell or lecture. Not only is it not effective, but yelling and shouting will have negative effects on the parent-child relationship.

• It doesn't matter "who started it," because it takes two to make a quarrel. As such, don't waste time trying to dig deep to find out who started each squabble; rather, focus on moving forward to find the right solution. Be consistent about this.

• Sometimes humour is the best medicine. Try to find something funny about the situation at hand and make a joke about it. This can easily defuse the conflict and may end up with everybody laughing. Be careful and make sure that the joke is not perceived as you picking on one of the children. Keep your jokes general and gender neutral.

• Promote empathy, understanding and compassion.

• Ignore small issues; address big ones. Learn how to overlook minor issues and focus on important matters that may leave your children feeling resentment or have a long term negative impact on their relationship

• Children do not have to be treated equally. Although parents should try to be fair with their children, there are times and circumstances where you may have to treat them differently. Take into consideration the age of the child, her ability, the circumstances around the incident at hand, etc.

• Every child is a favourite (refuse to hold up one child as a role model). Parents should be able to find each child's special talent, enhance it, and promote it.

• Time share. Togetherness is very important and to be able to spend time together with each child, try to get them involved while you are doing other activities.

Q. 10

We are a very conservative family and we try our best to raise our children as good Muslims. I have problems with one of my daughters who started high school this year and is currently in grade nine. As you know, in high school, many girls wear make up. One day she asked me if she could wear make up to school like the other girls. I was shocked and responded by telling her, 'how you dare ask me something like this? You know better. Of course you can't wear make up to the school.' She didn't take no for an answer. She said, 'Why not? Other girls at school wear make up. What is wrong with wearing make up?' I became upset and frustrated, and started shouting at her, telling her she was Muslim and she couldn't do things like this. She went back to her room and slammed the door. For the next week or so she was very angry with me, didn't want to eat dinner with the family, and stayed most of the time in her room when she was at home. One morning, she came downstairs, and to my surprise, she was wearing lipstick. I was shocked and asked her what she thought she was doing, and if she actually thought I'd let her go to school like that. I told her to go upstairs at once and clean her face before going to school. She shouted back saying, 'This is too much. I can't live in this house like this anymore. I'm not going to remove the lipstick. I'll go to school this way.' At this point, I blocked the door so she couldn't leave the house and ordered her to go upstairs again. She went upstairs to her room and slammed the door again and didn't go to school that day.

The tension between me and her now is very high and I don't know what to do. My question to you is whether I did the right thing preventing her from going out wearing lipstick, or not. Is it wrong to say no to our teens when they do things like this? If what I did is not proper can you please suggest a better way for me to be able to handle these kinds of situations in the future?

Answer   This is a very important question and we thank the sister for giving us enough details to help us in providing as much analysis as we can in our answer. We hope the following points respond to most if not all the issues that were raised in the question:

• After the first time your daughter asked you about wearing l ipstick, you mentioned that "I became upset and frustrated, and started shouting at her, telling her she was Muslim and she couldn't do things like this." This is not the correct way to deal with your children. A parent yelling has a very negative effect on the wellbeing of the children, as well as on the relationship between parents and children. In addition to humiliating the child, research proves that yelling affects the emotional health of the child; it lowers the child's self esteem, and affects her confidence negatively.

• To be able to raise your children properly, you need be in control of your actions with them. Yelling and shouting is not a sign of control at all. "It was reported on the authority of Abu Huraira, *RAA* that the messenger of Allah, *SAAW*, said, 'The strong person is not that who wrestles but the strong person is the one who controls himself in a fit of rage.'"[36]

• We don't really know what you mean by very conservative family in your question, and as such we will fall back on our experience in this area. In the past, while counseling other families who described themselves as conservative, we found out that they put lots of emphasis on the amount of knowledge their children have about Islam, such as how much Qur'an they memorize and how many *Ahadeeth* of Prophet Muhammad *SAAW* they know, which we feel is very important. However, at the same time, they neglected to give the opportunity to their children to ingrain this knowledge in their hearts and souls and make it part of their identity. They failed to make their children internalize this knowledge and elevate them to the level of

---

[36] Agreed upon

conviction. Providing a loving, warm, caring, and positive family atmosphere, discussing issues, and gently answering questions about the children's concerns are some of the very effective tools in achieving this conviction level.[37]

• When you want your child to do something, or not to do something, it is not enough just to say 'you should not do this because you are a Muslim'. The immediate reaction that comes to the mind of your teen is that Islam is just a bunch of restrictions for no obvious reasons. That is why it is very important to try to gently provide the logical reasons for the matters you want your child to follow.

• In addition to the previous points, the use of dialogue with your teen is very important. Allowing your teen to express herself freely and ask any questions she may have without fear of being rejected or reprimanded is without a doubt a main key to a successful relationship with your child. Of course, this can't be done without having an open channel of communication between you and your teen that is built on trust and understanding.

• Now, let us see how you as a mother should have responded to the situation when your daughter came downstairs and wanted to go to school wearing lipstick. This approach can also be used in the future if she tries the same thing again:

---

[37] See chapter 5 of our book **Muslim Teens, Today's Worry, Tomorrow's Hope**, published by amana publications for more details on how to help your teen achieve this convection

- Control your anger and put a smile on your face, greeting your daughter with a hug, and saying, 'good morning sweetie. You look so beautiful wearing this lipstick.' This comment is going to help relax the atmosphere and make your daughter more open to listen to what you will say next.

- You may like to continue in the same tone and pretend you don't understand what's going on, saying something like 'what is going on today? Are you experimenting with make up? Is this an experiment you require to do in your class?' Your daughter's answer of course will be, 'no mom I would like to wear lipstick to school today.'

- Keep your calm and say to her in a gentle voice, 'and why would you like to do this now?' Her answer will most likely be, 'most of the girls in class are doing it. Why not me? I would like to be like them. I don't think there is anything wrong with doing this.'

- Get her close to you and give her another hug, saying, "Sweetie, I totally understand that you want to be like the other girls at school, but you know that we don't do things just because others are doing them. We do things because they are the right thing to do. As you know, there is a proper place and proper time for everything. I don't think school is the right place to wear lipstick, nor is the classroom the proper time for it. And I'm sure that not all the girls in the classroom are wearing lipstick either." It may be a good idea at this point to suggest to your daughter inviting some of her friends over to have a make up party where they can try on different make up at home, and that this would be the right time for her to wear lipstick. Providing alternatives is one of the techniques Prophet Muhammad *SAAW* used to help Muslims give up certain unacceptable habits. "When the prophet, *SAAW*, came to Madinah, he found that they had two days of celebration and feasts. He told them that Allah had replaced these two days for them with two better days, the two Eids, Eid ul Adhha and Eidul Fitr." [38]

- After this dialogue with her, she might react in one of the following ways:

• She could say OK mom and wash off the lipstick before going to school. If this is the case, *alhamdulellah* the problem is solved. Don't forget to make *sujood Alshoker* to Allah *SWT*.

• She may resist a little and may need more convincing, saying, 'but Mom, I just want to try it one time. I want to do it today.' In this case, just give her a long affectionate hug and say, "Sweetie, you are too precious for me to let you go to school like this" and take her upstairs to help her wash off the lipstick. Reaffirm to her that as soon as she wants she can invite some friends over for her make up party.

We think the above approach is much more effective in resolving the problem. In addition, it is a gentle approach, as recommended by the Prophet Muhammad *SAAW* and loved by Allah *SWT*. Here are some *ahadeeth* that attest to this concept of kindness and gentleness:

---

[38] Muslim

• "On the authority of A'isha *RAA*, (beloved wife of the Prophet,) may Allah be pleased with her, she reported that the messenger of Allah, *SAAW*, said: Allah is gentle and kind and He loves kindness and gentleness in all affairs."[39]

• "Also she reported that the messenger of Allah, *SAAW*, had said: Allah is gentle and kind and He loves kindness; and confers upon kindness which He does not confer upon severity and does not confer upon anything else besides it (kindness)."[40]

• "On the authority of A'isha, may Allah be pleased with her, she reported that the messenger of Allah, *SAAW*, had said: Kindness is not found in anything but adds beauty to it, and if it is withdrawn from anything it defects it."[41]

• "On the authority of Gareer ibn Abdullah, may Allah be pleased with him, he reported that he heard the messenger of Allah, *SAAW*, saying: He who is deprived of leniency is deprived of good."[42]

• "On the authority of Ibn Abbas, may Allah be pleased with him, he reported that he heard the messenger of Allah, *SAAW*, saying to Ashaj Abdul Qais, may Allah be pleased with him: You posses two such qualities that Allah loves. These are forbearance and leniency."[43]

---

[39] Agreed Upon
[40] Muslim
[41] Muslim
[42] Muslim
[43] Muslim

We also would like to affirm that we are not promoting to parents to cave in to their children's desires and allow them to do what they want. To the contrary, we think parents should allow their children to do the right things only, but they should do it tactfully through discussions and dialog with their children. An upfront 'NO' and direct confrontation makes the situation more tense and will negatively affect the relationship between parents and their children.

Q. 11

I'm writing on behalf of myself and my wife. We have a big concern regarding our middle child, who is a grade 8 student whose name is Ziyad. We also have an older son who is 16 years old whose name is Ahmad and a younger daughter Fatima who is 9 years old. Ziyad is a nice boy who gets along with his brother and sister. He is also nice and polite to me and my wife. He gets along with his classmates and has friends at school and in our neighborhood. However, Ziyad doesn't put enough effort into his schoolwork and his average grade on his report card is 'C'. Ziyad is on good terms with his brother and looks up to him, but even though his older brother is a straight 'A' student, Ziyad doesn't get motivated by this or try to follow in his brother's footsteps with regards to his studies. We have tried different methods to get him to improve: We've written a contract with him, where we agreed that he would not get to go out and play street hockey with his friend until he finished school work. However, my wife feels bad about it and usually allows him to go out to play before finishing his homework. When she realizes that this behavior is not helping, she says, 'this is the last time I will do this.' We are concerned about his education in the long term, and how this will affect his college options when he gets older. We believe he has high potential to excel in school if he puts his mind to it, and all his teachers agree. Is there anything that we can do so he has a better opportunity regarding his education?

Answer   From the details in your question, it doesn't look like Ziyad has a learning disability, and he has no problem with concentration or focus since his parents and teachers agree that he has good potential to excel in school if he puts his mind to it. As such, our advice for his parents will be to basically do two things. These are:

1. Evaluate Ziyad's physical situation and environmental conditions. Make sure they are proper and that they are helping him to do an acceptable job with his academics. The areas to check are his sleep and dietary habits. Does he regularly get enough sleep? Is he eating a healthy, wholesome, and suitable diet for his age and the level of activities he is involved in? These are questions that parents have to honestly answer, and try to modify his dietary habits and adjust his sleep patterns to make sure they are contributing positively to the improvement of his school work rather than hindering his progress

2. Teach him good work ethic. Not all children are created to be straight A students. As such, our criteria of success shouldn't be the grades achieved by Ziyad. Instead, it should be making sure that he is reaching his potential as far as studying and school-work is concerned. This can only be done by teaching him good

work habits, and making sure that the home environment is conducive for him to follow these good work habits. Among these good work habits is that when he comes home form the school, he relaxes for 15 to 20 minutes with a light snack, then starts his homework. Also, he may take reasonable breaks to refresh himself. Reviewing homework before submitting it is another good work habit. To further help him, the home should be quiet during homework time and other kids shouldn't be doing something really tempting, like watching TV at the same time.

Here is how parents should proceed:

• Parents should work together as a team and first, both of them should agree on a plan and come up with a course of action to follow with Ziyad.

• Have a meeting with Ziyad to explain the rules to him that will be applied regarding organizing his time in general. In addition to homework and other house chores, parents should make sure to include Ziyad's sports hobbies. Negotiating a contract could be a very useful tool in such situations.[44]

• Follow up closely on a daily basis and be consistent in applying the agreed upon rules and terms of the contract. Follow up charts are important and provide an effective tool that helps in monitoring the progress.[45]

• It is of utmost importance to remind the parents not to compare Ziyad with his other siblings.

---

[44] See the section on (Behavioural Contract) in chapter 9 of our book **Muslim Teens, Today's Worry, Tomorrow's Hope,** published by amana publications for details on how to write the contract, terms of the contract, and the conditions to be taken into consideration to ensure the success of the contract

[45] You can come up with your own follow up charts, or use the suggested charts in the previous reference

I hope this message finds you in the best of health and eemaan. I have 3 daughters ages 8, 6, and 3. We live in North America. I write to you as I am very concerned about the behavior I am seeing from my eldest daughter mainly, but also to some extent from the other 2 girls.

The eldest is very defiant; she will not listen to things she is asked to do, even the smallest things such as going to the bathroom, picking something up, helping with cleaning up, etc. She will ignore us completely, as though she hasn't even heard us ask her, and when I repeat a request a few times over, she will just shout out 'I heard you' or 'I know'.

She has become very rude towards me, even making faces, answering back, and shouting at me regularly. She will also shout and be rude to the other 2 siblings by screaming at the top of her lungs to them, saying things like I told you not to touch my things, get out of my way, I hate you, move, stop staring at me. She will even physically push them. They will start this kind of behavior in the morning.

I am puzzled as to what I have done wrong. Ever since they were very young, we would always start the day with dua and Quran first. We do not have a TV in the house. The older 2 were home schooled for 2 years and have started Islamic school this year. They are also doing hifdh of Quran. They have been doing Islamic studies with me since they were very young and I try to teach them the duas for different occasions. They do not behave like this with their father or others.

We have started a chore chart with 'mom and dad dollars'. We have a sticker tree for good behaviour. I told them that when it became full, they could have some friends over for a pizza party. They receive small candy points when they offer the prayers on time or complete reading Quran homework, or listen the first time.

I am making dua always that Allah may forgive me, help me, and protect my children in every way. I am trying to pinpoint my mistakes and use different ways.

Any advice would be greatly appre-

*ciated. Jazakumullah Khair for taking
the time to read this message. May you
be rewarded the best of dunya and
even more Aakhirah. Please make dua
for us.*

Answer   This is a compounded question and there are many
issues to be addressed. Although the mother tried her best to give us as
much information as possible, we would have loved to get more details
on specific issues related to the reaction of the children to home schooling and their *hifdh* program, as well as how the parents react to the
defiant behavior of the eldest daughter, and what kind of discipline
mechanisms they have used with her in these situations. In the absence
of this kind of information we will try our best to provide some advice
based on our understanding of the problem, and while making certain
assumptions based on our experience with other families whom we have
counseled for similar problems. Here are a few tips that we hope will
help in rectifying the situation:

- It looks like you have a very structured life and you are
  stressed out with trying to achieve so many things. We suggest
  that you re-evaluate the programs you have with your children
  and see if they need any adjustment. Ask yourself what your
  goal is for each activity you have for your children and make
  sure that these goals are within the ability of the children to
  achieve. For example, we believe that a Muslim's goal for a
  Qur'anic memorization program (*hifdh*) should be to make
  the children love Qur'an: get into the habit of reading it, understanding it, and memorizing parts of it. The portion to be
  memorized will differ from one child to the other because not

all children have the same ability for memorization. As such, when we develop a *hifdh* program for a child, we should take into consideration the child's ability for memorization, the available time, other programs in place for this child, and the time needed for play and relaxation according to the child's age. It is much better to raise a child who memorizes a smaller portion of Qur'an but who is in the habit of memorizing more Qur'an on her own than to raise a child who memorizes a bigger portion of Qur'an but is at risk of abandoning it as soon as she is on her own, because she feels that she was robbed of her childhood by her parents, who forced her to spend lots of time in memorization without providing enough bonding and entertainment time.

• It also seems like the relationship between you and your older daughter is seriously strained, to say the least. This could be the result of many years of your giving her massive doses of instructions and discipline, without building a strong emotional bond between you and the children. Because of this, your daughter may perceive you as the policeperson of the family and that may explain why she is not being rude with your husband. There is a great need for you to rebuild the relationship between yourself and your children. This could be achieved by doing the following:

- Chart your own self. Try to find out how many times you correct and instruct your daughter. If you find out that you do this excessively, try to reduce it. Also find out how you respond to her requests. Do you say 'no' a lot to her? Can you replace any of these with 'yes's instead?

- Conduct the "Self Search Process" [46] on yourself to find out the sources of your own negative parental behaviors, which may be contributing negatively to the relationship between you and your daughter.

- Make a commitment that you will try to get rid of these short-comings and replace them with other habits that will contribute positively to your relationship with your daughter.

- Re-evaluate all the chores and activities your children are involved in as described in the above point.

- Start a new program for your children's activities that is not only focused on chores and achievements, but also takes into account their entertainment and play time needs.

- Make sure that you allocate at least 20-30 minute blocks of play and bonding time 2-3 times a day within this program.

- Work with your husband as a team. Agree together on your discipline plan and make sure he participates in executing it with you, or even on his own when the need arises.

• List all of your daughter's unacceptable behaviors that you want to correct. Don't try to work on all of them at once. Pick the three most important ones that you want to tackle first and deal with them one by one.

---

[46] See our book *Parenting Skills according to Qur'an and Sunnah* published by amana publications for the details of the "Self Search Process"

• We recommend using the "Indicate, Educate, and Train Methodology"[47] to correct the targeted behavior of your daughter.

• Don't expect immediate results. Be ready to repeat the process more than once and be patient. Changing behavior is a process and requires time.

• Celebrate each and every success with your daughter.

We hope the above tips will help improve the situation *insha'a* Allah.

---

[47] See the previous reference for the details of "Indicate, Educate, and Train Methodology" as well as the answer of question number 14 in this book

Hello. I have a problem with my son that I know I caused by neglecting him when he was young. My husband and I are not good at parenting, or at least we want to be good parents but just don't know how and find it very hard. I think this is because I grew up in a family where nobody ever cared about anybody but themselves. My mother never told me to do my homework, never checked if I had eaten, and never even talked or played with me. She was always busy with her problems and did not care about us in anyway, but would always claim that she loved us very much. So I guess I grew up to be like her in so many ways, even by claiming that I love my kids but basically neglecting them, being there physically with them at home but not being there emotionally at all. My husband has always been very mean and uninvolved with our family. I've felt that he doesn't care about the kids or I because he doesn't make time for us. He's always working 7 days a week and when it comes to his break in the summer he travels to visit his family in Egypt, leaving us at home. I have four kids, ages 11, 9, 7 and 5. The 3 older

children are boys, and the 5 year-old is a girl. Since Hasaneen, my oldest, was born I have neglected him, as I was suffering from depression. I used to hit him and ignore him just like my mother did with me. This continued until Hasaneen turned 10, when he started to hit me back and curse at me. At that point I basically made a 180 degree turn in my attitude: I insisted that we move to a State that has Islamic schools for the kids, and after one year of trying to move, I finally left my home and my husband and moved with the kids. Then after six month my husband came to live with us but he didn't have a job, so he stayed home. When he was around them all the time, he started to want to be involved in the parenting, and he was very strict, so my oldest son started to curse at him very badly and show no respect at all. He also plays violent video games, refuses to eat, and continues to curse at me all the time, calling me bad mother. I tried to tell him I would buy him different video games that do not contain violence he refused and just wants to play the same violent game. I've also tried to stop him from drinking coke, but he became very violent and screamed and refused. He insists on eating only Chinese takeout, and chocolate milk all the time. When I tell him to eat the food I cooked, he will refuse to eat all day. He is very polite to his teacher and to me as long as I don't tell him what to do. Ever since he started going to Islamic school, he has started to pray and believe in god and respect Islam in many ways. I took him to the Masjid where his friend was talking about respect toward parents, and how it is very bad to disrespect your parents but he still disrespects me all the time. What can I do? I know it is my fault but I hope it is not too late to help correct his behavior. My husband wants to send him boarding school in Canada where they are all Muslim in the hopes that this will improve his behavior, but I think this will make him hate us even more.

Answer Thank you very much for contacting us regarding this problem. First, let me congratulate you for taking this step and realizing that you could be part of the reason for your son's ill behavior. Most probably, your son's bad behaviour is a result of years of neglect and/or uninformed parenting techniques that are not based on knowledge. This is a compound problem and the solution may require many counselling sessions with a professional Muslim Counsellor. In the absence of such a counsellor, you need to work on three major fronts. The first of them is comprehensive knowledge consisting of Islamic knowledge in general, Islamic parenting knowledge, knowledge of the developmental stages of children at various ages, and knowledge of your children's environment. The second front is that of wisdom. Although some wisdom is a gift from Allah *SWT* to some of His servants[48], a great portion of wisdom can be acquired through knowledge, since our beloved Prophet Muhammad *SAAW* has said, "Wisdom (good practices) is the goal of a believer. Wherever he finds it he should pick it up and use it."[49] You will need wisdom in many situations such as making the right decision on how to parent your child properly, on how much of your ethnic culture should be practiced by your child, and in understanding that not all children are the same and that you may have to emphasize different issues with different children and so on. The third front is that of exerting effort. To learn all this kinds of knowledge and to provide a better alternative for your children, you and your husband will have to exert lots of effort. The following are some suggested recommendations on how you and your husband can proceed insha'a Allah:

First: To find out the sources of negative parental bahvior you and your husband have, we would recommend that both of you conduct the Self Search. This will help both of you in identifying your parenting shortcomings and strengths. Make a list of the three most serious shortcomings and make a commitment to avoid using them with your children, and to try to replace them with more positive parenting methods. Here is how you conduct the Self Search:

---

[48] Q 2, V 269)
[49] Ibn Majjah

Self Search and Self Improvement process

This is the process of holding oneself accountable for what he or she is doing and trying to correct one's actions to get the best results in any given area of life. This process is a central theme in Islam and is recommended by verses of Qur'an and sayings of Prophet Muhammad *SAAW* as well as practices of his companions.[50] This process consists of six steps. These are: search, evaluate, acknowledge, reinforce, change, and hang on. Let us now elaborate on each of these steps:

Search within ourselves and review all the actions and parental behaviors that we use with our children. We must dig deep into our past, thinking back to childhood, and uncover any hidden reasons that might be the source of our parental behavior. Often, we may be talking to our children in a certain way, and if we stopped to think about it, we would realize that we are doing exactly what our mom or dad used to do with us.

Evaluate the actions and sayings we use in dealing with our children. Which of these actions are positive, supportive, and based on Islamic values and teachings, and which of these actions are negative, unsupportive, and have no basis in Islamic teachings? An example of a negative action is when we, as parents, try to resolve a conflict with our child while we are angry. If we yell, shout, and fight with the child just to vent our anger, we are using a negative parental behavior. However, if

---

[50] Consult with our book *Parenting Skills according to Qur'an and Sunnah* amana publications, Beltsville, MD, 2004 for further information on evidence of the process from Qur'an and teachings of Prophet Muhammad *SAAW*

we control our anger by using the anger management techniques prescribed to us by our beloved Prophet *SAAW*, teach our child to do the same, and then discuss the problem calmly, we are using a positive parental behavior.[51]

Acknowledge our findings and categorize them as either positive or negative behaviors. Again, the positive ones are those that agree with Islamic teachings, are suitable for the environment, and help our children become strong and confident Muslims. The negative behaviors are those that are mainly from inherited tradition, have no basis in Islamic teachings, may not be suitable for the environment, and may make our children feel defeated as Muslims. Acknowledging our strengths and weaknesses is the first step in improving our parental behavior. After that, we have to put our trust in Allah *SWT* and make a commitment to positive change. Changing unhealthy habits is the key to success, as the great scholar Ibn al-Qayyim said, "and the core of the matter is in leaving out the unhealthy, inherited habits."

Reinforce the positive parental behaviors and keep practicing them with our children. If they work, we must continue using them.

Change the negative parental behaviors and replace them with positive ones. We have to work hard at this because change does not come easily. It takes hard work to change habits, so we have

---

[51] See the previous reference for many practical examples on negative and positive parental behaviours

to be patient and keep trying. Changing bad habits into good ones is worth the struggle. The expected benefits in our children's development are too important for us not to try our best to change these habits. When trying to change our bad habits or negative parenting behavior, we should follow the advice of the Prophet *SAAW* and always perform *salat-ul-hajah*, the prayer of need, and make *du'a* intensively, to help us in the process of trying to become better parents. In addition, we must repeat this prayer several times, rather than just performing it once.

Hang On We cannot give up right away. We should put our trust in Allah and keep trying. As parents, we can learn new ways and improve on our old ways. The positive results will be certain if we follow the above steps. It may take longer than we think, but we can't give up. The reward will be tremendous if we work hard and make a sincere effort to become better parents.[52]

While doing this self search process, we emphasize again that we consistently seek Allah's support through regular and intensive *du'a* to help us achieve our goals. We also seek Allah's help to strengthen us by doing *Salatul-Hajah*.[53]

Second: There are many Islamic parenting principles that every Muslim parent should learn to help them parent their children

---

[52] For more information about the self-search process and practical examples of positive and negative parental behaviours, please see **Parenting Skills According to Qur'an and Sunnah** By Drs. Ekram & Mohamed Beshir, amana publications, Beltsville, MD, 2004

[53] *Salatul-Hajah* is a prayer for a need. The Prophet *SAAW* recommended that if you need the help of Allah in any matter, you try your best and seek His help via performing two *Raka'h* of prayer to Allah and making a certain *Du'aa/* asking Allah to help you with this specific matter

properly and achieve the required results. Among them is linking the child to Allah, understanding your child and parenting with knowledge, understanding your child's environment, providing a healthy, pleasant, loving, and positive family atmosphere, expressing love, gentleness, and kindness, sharing feelings, practicing mutual respect, bonding on a personal level with each child, emphasizing positive action, providing positive peer pressure, and working toward a common point of reference .[54] Try to learn as many as you can from these Islamic parenting principles. Your focus should mainly be on some of the key Islamic parenting principles that are suitable for the age of your son, such as knowledge, wisdom, effective communication, teaching and training children for accountability, responsibility, and respectability; providing healthy and suitable alternatives, being consistent, and providing a healthy, pleasant, loving and positive family atmosphere.

Third: Make a list of your son's bad behaviors that you want to change. Pick the three most serious of them to work on one by one to help your son getting rid of his bad behavior. Don't try to change many behaviors at the same time as this will be too difficult for him.

Fourth: Learn the proper/positive way of changing your son's behavior using the "Indicate, Educate, and Train Technique" [55]

---

[54] For a more exhaustive list of these principles, please consult with our book *When Muslim Teens Rebel: Causes and Solutions*, amana publications, 2008.

[55] See our book *Parenting Skills According to Qur'an and Sunnah*. amana publications, Beltsville, MD, 2004

and try to apply it with each of the three identified bad behaviors. You may have to repeat the trial more than once. Be patient and don't expect immediate change. It is a process and it takes time, but results are usually positive if we apply the technique properly.

The above recommendations may seem overwhelming; however, if you start taking the initiative and seeking Allah's help with regular and continuous *du'a* you will see results *insha'a* Allah soon. Also, we would like to emphasize that the above recommendations can be done concurrently. You don't have to finish step one and then start step two and so on. You can do more than one of the above recommendation at the same time.

As for sending your child to a boarding school in Canada, it is very difficult to comment on this idea and to know if it is a good or a bad one without thorough knowledge of this school, their staff, and their program. We suggest that you do intensive home-work before making a decision. Visit the school and get to know the teachers and the administrative staff and their qualifications. Focus on their knowledge of how to deal with children and adolescents. Ask questions and try to make sure they are quali-fied in this area. This is the most important area where it will make a difference in the manners and characters of your child. It will be also beneficial to you if you can find some parents who enrolled their children in this school or other Islamic board-ing schools, and try to learn from their experience. Ask them all the questions you have in your mind before finalizing your decision.

Q.14

My son is 15 years old. Sometimes when he's talking with me, he raises his voice in a rude way. This really upsets me, so I end up yelling at him not to that. I usually threaten him, either with depriving him of his allowance or cutting his computer hours. This situation happens frequently. Is there a better way to handle this situation?

Answer   As we indicated in the answer of question 10, parents should not yell and shout at their children, due to the negative effects it has on the children, as well as their relationship with their parents. In addition, yelling and shouting are not effective in correcting behavior. You can see this even in the fact that, as you indicated in your question, the situation occurs frequently. Does this mean that we shouldn't correct the improper behavior of our children? Of course not. It is our duty as parents to take all necessary steps to correct any bad behavior we notice with our children, particularly if this behavior has to do with an important concept in Islam such as respecting others.

We recommend the use of the "Indicate, Educate, and Train" technique. This is a recommended Islamic method for correcting and changing a child's negative behavior. We would like to emphasize that for this technique to work effectively, the user has to be in charge and control her emotions, remaining calm and assertive through out. The technique consists of the following three main steps:

1. **Indicate** clearly to the child his mistake or unacceptable be-

havior in a calm but firm manner. For example, in your case, your teen was being disrespectful by speaking to an older person (his mother) loudly and in a rude tone of voice. Give him the benefit of the doubt and assume that the child didn't know better, and then indicate to him that this behavior is not acceptable. Do this by using an appropriate comment that suits the child's age, and speaking with a firm tone of voice that is calm and not angry. It is important to emphasize here that this should be done in a very respectful way, to set an example and to show the child how you want him to behave.

2. **Educate** the child about the issue at hand using verses from the Qur'an and teachings of the Prophet Muhammad *SAAW*. For example, when responding to disrespect, you can mention the following saying of the Prophet Muhammad *SAAW*:

"The one who does not have mercy on our young ones and does not show respect to our elders is not one of us." [56]

Using verses from the Qur'an and the teachings of the Prophet *SAAW* helps the child understand that our ultimate reference is to the orders of Allah *SWT*, and that even parents are expected to adhere to these orders. This will also help parents avoid confrontations with their children. It removes the factors that cause power struggles, since the parents are not making up the rules and imposing them on the children, but actually, both the parents and children are following Allah's rules.

---

[56] At-Termithy

3. **Train** the child to frequently practice the correct behavior in the proper way, with your guidance. Do not expect that by following these steps once, the child will behave appropriately all the time and not repeat the mistake. You need to repeat the process each time the child repeats the mistake or behaves in an unacceptable way. You may have to do it several times until it becomes a habit for the child. Training and practice makes perfect.

For more examples and a detailed explanation of this technique, we refer the reader to our book *Parenting Skills based on Qur'an and Sunnah.*[57]

---

[57] Beshir, Dr. Ekram and Dr. Mohamed Rida, ***Parenting Skills based on the Qur'an and Sunnah***, first edition. Beltsville, Maryland: amana publications, 2004

ACHIEVEMENT, QUR'ANIC MEMORIZATION AND PRAYER TRAINING

Q.15. *My son is 7 years old and we always motivate him to do well at school and try his best to be a top student. I notice lately that he has started pointing out at other children in the family or friends, and saying that they know nothing and that they are not as good as him. Should I be concerned? If yes, what to do?*

Q.16. *My son is 9 years old. Masha'a Allah he has a strong memory and a good voice. My husband and I are always keen about him memorizing Qur'an. Our son is doing well in his memorization and he is always a top student in Qur'anic programs. He is usually chosen to recite Qur'an at the beginning of community activities. Lately my son has made a few comments where he puts other kids down for not being as good as him in Qur'anic recitation. I was not happy to hear him speak this way, but didn't know how to handle it, as we didn't want him not to lose his enthusiasm for Qur'an memorization.*

Q.17. My nephew is 8 years old. He is very smart and memorizes lots of Qur'an. He is also doing well at school and receives lots of achievement awards. He is usually chosen to recite Qur'an as an opening for various school functions. His grandfather has a lot to do with his excellence in Qur'anic memorization since he spends a lot of time teaching and reviewing with him. He feels very proud of his grandchild. He always tells him 'you are the best' and favors him over the rest of the family children. Lately, and more than once, I have overheard him telling his cousin, 'I'm better than you and you can never be as good as I am. You see all these awards are mine and I also memorize much more Qur'an than you.' I was puzzled by what I heard. I feel that something needs to be corrected there. Please advise.

Answer   These are three questions that share a very important concept for us as Muslims. It is very important to make sure that our children understand this concept very clearly. The concept we are referring to is that of the purity of intentions and motives behind our actions (*neyah*). It was reported by Omar Ibn Al Khattab *RAA* that Prophet Muhammad *SAAW* has said, "Deeds are judged based on the motives behind them. Those who migrate for Allah and His messenger, their migration will be counted as such. And those who migrate to achieve some worldly gain or marry a specific lady, their migration also will be counted as such."[58]

In another very vivid saying of Prophet Muhammad *SAAW*, it was also reported by Aby Hurairah *RAA* that Prophet Muhammad *SAAW* has said, "The first three people who will be thrown into Hellfire are a martyr (*Shaheed*), a generous wealthy person, and a scholar. Allah will remind the martyr about the bounties and blessings that He bestowed on him and will ask him, 'What did you do with these bounties and blessings?' The martyr will say, 'I used them and fought for your cause until I died.' Allah *SWT* will answer, 'No, you fought so people would say that you were a brave person and they said so. As such your abode is Hellfire." And the martyr will be thrown into Hellfire. Then Allah *SWT* will remind the generous wealthy person about the bounties and blessings that He bestowed on him and will ask him, 'What did you do with these bounties and blessings?' The generous wealthy person will say, 'I used them to help the poor and needy, and I donated my wealth in various charities for your cause.' Allah *SWT* will answer, 'No, you donated so people would say you were a generous person, and they said so. As such your abode is Hellfire.' And the generous wealthy person will be thrown into Hellfire. Then Allah *SWT* will remind the scholar about the bounties and blessings that He bestowed on him and will ask him, 'What did you do with these bounties and blessings?' The scholar will say, 'I used the knowledge to teach people and all of this was in your cause.' Allah *SWT* will answer, 'No, you taught people so they would say you were a

---

[58] Agreed upon

knowledgeable person and they said so. As such your abode is Hellfire.'
And the scholar will be thrown into Hellfire." [59]

Use the above two sayings of Prophet Muhammad *SAAW* to warn those
boys that their actions may not be accepted at all because they are not
doing them for the right reasons. Boasting and putting other kids down
are major sins for which we can be punished. On the other hand, doing
things with the proper intentions guarantees and ensures that Allah *SWT*
may look favorably on our actions, and that we will be rewarded for
them *insha'a* Allah. As such, they should stop boasting and looking
down on other kids so they will get the full reward for their actions.

Also remind them that the beautiful voice and strong memory they have
are given to them as a gift from Allah *SWT* and that they should use
them properly. They should be thankful to Him, and the best way to
demonstrate this thankful attitude is to use Allah's bounties properly
and not to make them a source of annoyance, disgrace, embarrassment,
and humiliation for other Muslim children.

Talk to the Islamic activities organizers in your community and
request of them not to always choose those boys to recite Qur'an at the
beginning of community activities. Ask them to alternate and use other
children in the community. I'm sure there must be other community
children who have some Qur'an memorized and would be able to recite
at the openings of activities. Putting your children excessively in the
spotlight may not be the best thing for their wellbeing and emotional
development.

---

[59] Muslim

In the case of question 17, there is no doubt that the grandfather is contributing to the negative behavior of his grandchild. It is very important that parents of your nephew talk to the grandfather in a very gentle and respectable way about this issue. This is not going to be an easy thing to do, and as such parents, have to be very tactful and soft in their approach with the grandfather. Here is how we suggest they go about it:

- Choose a suitable time when the grandfather is relaxed and in a good mood to open up the subject with him

- Thank the grandfather for his generosity in taking care of their son, his continuous encouragement, and for the effort he puts into making their son love the Qur'an and memorize a good part of it. Make sure to indicate that it is with Allah's blessings and the grandfather's follow up, support, dedication, and providing the right model that their son is where he is right now.

- Mention a few of the incidents where the boy was boasting and bragging to his cousins and putting them down.

- Request the help of the grandfather to solve this problem and ask him if he can provide any advice, since he has a wealth of experience that could help in such situations.

- The grandfather may suggest on his own to reduce the amount of praise given to the boy by the adults in his life as part of his advice.

- If he doesn't make this suggestion, subtly bring it up in a form of a question, such as, "Do you think reducing the amount of praise given to him by the adults in his life would help in correcting his negative attitude?"

• Hopefully, the grandfather will get the hint, realize the severity of the situation, and start trying to reduce his praise towards the child and be a part of the solution *insha'a* Allah.

 *I'm having problem teaching my 6 year-old child to keep up with his prayers. Is there any advice you can provide or methods I can use to make sure he performs his prayers regularly?*

Answer Training our children for prayer is an important and noble duty for each and every Muslim parent. It is an order from Allah *SWT* that we have to enjoin our family members with prayer and be constant in doing this[60]. The Prophet *SAAW* also emphasized this in his very famous saying: "Teach your children to perform *Salah* when they are seven years old and hit them if they do not do it when they are ten years old."[61] We commend the sister for her efforts to provide this very important training for her child. For this training to be effective and yield the best results *insha'a* Allah, we recommend the following to be taken into consideration:

• Before the age of seven, training children to pray should be done mainly via modeling, and including the child in the activities done by the family.

• Make sure you have an *Athaan* clock in the house and as soon as the *Athaan* is called, stop any activities you are doing and tell all your kids to stop what they are doing and get ready for the prayer.

---

[60] Q20, V132)

[61] Abu Dawoud and At-Termithy

• Depending on the child's age, show those who are still young how to make *wudoo'* and get ready for the prayer. Those who are older will do their *wudoo'* and join the group.

• Always do the *salat* in congregation.

• As soon as the child turns 7 years old, have a meeting with him or her to discuss serious commitments to performing *salat*. Get the child to agree to make at least one *salat* every day. Help her to select one of the five daily prayers not to miss at all; say *Asr* prayer for example. Include this in her follow-up chart where she collects points every time she fulfills her duties with respect to various chores. As soon as the number of points reaches a certain agreed upon limit, she will have the right to redeem these points for a gift or something she likes.

• Follow up closely and make sure the child does not miss the specific, agreed upon *salat* every day. This will help him to understand the meaning of commitment and being consistent.

• When the child reaches eight years old, have a meeting again with him and express your happiness about his success in following and honoring his commitments to *salat*. Explain to him that it is time to increase this commitment and make sure that now, since he has turned eight years old, he will do at least two *salats* every day. Help him to decide which two salats he will do. *Asr* and *Maghreb* could be a good choice *insha'a* Allah.

• Again, follow up closely and make sure the child does not miss these two specific agreed upon salats every day. Update the follow up chart of the child to include these new commitments. Again, this will help the child to understand the meaning of commitment and being consistent.

• Continue using the same method with the target to reach five daily prayers by the time the child turns ten years old.

With the above step-by-step gradual approach, it is much easier for the child to learn how to be consistent with *salat insha'a* Allah. Remember that children have a short attention span and that they require constant follow up, including things like visual charts and frequent rewards to encourage them in continuing their progress. Whenever you can, also accompany this training with stories from the life of the companion of Prophet Muhammad *SAAW*, illustrating how they loved prayer and always tried to pray behind him.

Finally, for boys, it is very important that their dad takes them regularly with him to the *Masjid* for congregation prayer. Starting from 10 years old, if you live close to the *Masjid*, the father should accompany his son for at least one prayer a day or whenever it is possible. Depending on the time of the year, *Maghreb* or *Isha* prayer may be the most suitable prayers to perform in the Mosque *insha'a* Allah.

Q. 19

My son is seven years old. Masha'a Allah, he has learned how to read the short "Surahs" of the Qur'an and he has almost memorized the 30th chapter (Juz'). I try to get him to review what he has memorized every night for about half an hour after he finishes his homework and has dinner. As he can read on his own, I expect him to sit down and do it by himself, whether it is revision or new memorization. He is not responding well and is always fighting to get out of it. Is my expectation reasonable? What should I do?

Answer   There is no doubt that teaching our children Qur'an is a very noble cause and we should try our best to help them memorize as much as they can *insha'a* Allah. However, we believe that parents should keep in mind several things when setting up a *Qur'anic* memorization program for their children so that they help their children develop a love and appreciation of the Quran that will last their entire lifetime *insha'a* Allah. The goal is to help your children learn to love the Qur'an and love to get into the habit of reading it, understanding it, and memorizing parts of it. The portion to be memorized will differ from one child to the other because not all children have the same ability for memorization. As such, when developing a memorization program for a child, we should take into consideration the child's ability for memorization, the available time, other activities and programs in place for this child, and the amount of time needed for play and relaxation according to the child's age. It is much better to raise a child who has memorized a smaller portion of Qur'an but is consistent and committed to memorizing more on his own, than to raise a child who has memorized a bigger portion of Qur'an but is at risk of abandoning the Qur'an as soon as he is on his own because he feels like he was robbed of his childhood by his parents who forced him to spend lots of time memorizing the Quran without providing him with enough time to play and bond with his parents.

From your question and the resistance of your son, we detect that he may not be getting enough time to play and bond with you. We feel that at this age, it is not easy for a child to sit for long periods of time and focus on the memorization and revision of the Qur'an on his own.

We recommend that you re-evaluate his memorization program and make sure it is within his abilities. Replacing part of the memorization time with story telling about some verses of the Qur'an is one way of making the program more interesting for him. Furthermore, giving him explanations of the meanings of the memorized verses in a simple way that could touch his heart will have a much better and long lasting effect on your child's personality and character than just memorization alone. Make sure that your child has enough bonding and relaxation time during the day which will allow him to re-energize and be more enthusiastic for memorization. He needs to be motivated and he needs the follow up from both of you. The more balanced the program is and the more time you spend with him, the better the results will be *insha'a* Allah.

SCHOOLING AND ENVIRONMENT

Q.20

If peer acceptance and approval for teenagers is more important than parents, as you have indicated in many of your lectures and books, would you recommend moving children to Islamic schools during the high school years?

Answer   This is a very good question and, in order to answer it, we need to discuss in detail whose approval matters to children during the various stages of their life, as well as when and why we should move our children from one type of school to another.

First, it is a known fact that when it comes to approval, children will by default go through two main stages. During the first stage, which extends from birth to around ten years old, the approval of parents is most important to the children, as compared to other sources of approval. From approximately ten years old up to almost 19 years old, the approval of peers is most important to the teens, as compared to other sources of approval. Given the unacceptable norms of North American popular teen culture, in our books and lectures, we always recommend that parents invest properly during the first stage to avoid the negative effects of the second stage when teens are naturally drawn to fit in and be accepted by their peers.

It is important to elaborate here on what we mean by investing properly during first stage. Proper investment means using every opportunity, and using proper techniques, during this stage to instill important

Islamic concepts in the mind and heart of your child[62]. Your objective as a parent is to make sure that these concepts and values become part of your child's identity. It is not enough that your child memorizes certain *surahs* of Qur'an and sayings of the prophet *SAAW*; rather, the goal is for him to internalize the teachings of the *Qur'anic* verses and sayings of the prophet *SAAW* and have the conviction to live by them. To succeed in achieving this goal, you need to put the following three components in place:

• **Parent your child with knowledge.** This means you need to acquire the following types of knowledge:
- General Islamic Knowledge
- Islamic parenting principles and techniques based on Qur'an and the teachings of Prophet Muhammad *SAAW*
- Knowledge of children's developmental stages
- Knowledge of the environment that our children are living in, and interacting with day after day

Knowledge in the above described areas is a must for every parent, in order to be able to provide proper training to your child, and to ensure that she has strong faith and is proud of her identity as Muslim

• **Use wisdom in parenting:** Wisdom is a great asset. Parents need wisdom as well as knowledge, as knowledge in itself is

---

[62] See chapter 6 of Drs Ekram and Mohamed Rida Beshir; ***Muslim Teens: Today's Worry, Tomorrow's Hope***, amana publications, Beltsville, Maryland, USA, 2nd edition, third printing, 2007

not enough. Wisdom will help parents to apply their knowledge properly. Wisdom is a parent's best friend, particularly when dealing with teens. It is needed to handle each situation according to its own merits, and to make sure parents don't compare their children to each other. Children are not all the same and wisdom is needed to find out the key to each child's personality and the best way to deal with that personality. Wisdom is needed by parents to pick their fights and make sure they overlook minor mistakes by their teens to strengthen the bond between them and their children, rather than straining the relationship by being picky. Wisdom is also needed to know when to say "No" and when to say "Yes". Not only this, but it is also needed to know when to replace "No" with "Yes" whenever you can because too many "No's" may have a drastic effect on the relationship with your teen and on the way he views Islam. Wisdom is needed for parents to appreciate the different environment our teens are living in and the types of pressures they are facing in this environment. Wisdom is also needed to ensure that parents can see the bigger picture in every situation and try to always choose the lesser of the two evils, rather than being stubborn and causing more harm by straining their relationship with their teens and letting the situation slip out of their hands. Wisdom is not only a gift from Allah to some people, but can also be acquired, developed, and enhanced by individuals. The prophet *SAAW* said, "Wisdom is the goal of a believer, wherever he finds it he is the most deserving of gaining it."[63]

---

[63] Ibn Majah and At Termithy

• **Exerting effort:** To be able to acquire all these areas of knowledge and do what it takes to provide the proper training for your child, no doubt, you will need to exert effort. Effort is needed to start activities, drive your child to the location of these activities and provide healthy alternatives for them. It is needed to neutralize the default negative environment, reduce negative peer pressure and establish a positive support system for your teen. Parents should be willing to exert effort and do their best to help their teens.

Utilizing the above three components will no doubt help parents to make sure their children internalize various Islamic concepts and values, and that these values become part of their identity. A teen who is convinced with Islam as a way of life, has Islamic habits, believes in higher values, and mold her life according to these values will resist temptations from Western popular teen culture and be in a better position not to fall prey to negative behavior simply to fit in.

If parents succeed in bringing up teens with the above qualities, no matter which school they are attending, they will not compromise their values for the sake of being accepted. They will resist the temptation to be a follower for the sake of fitting in. As such, they will survive the pressure being in a public school and will not compromise their identity. Of course, having them enrolled in a good Islamic school is going to help in providing the support mechanisms needed, as well as the variety of activities to keep them strong and confident Muslims. One point we like to emphasize here is that some Islamic schools don't do enough in the way of activities in their curriculum to prepare their students to interact with confidence in a non-Islamic environment. It is of utmost importance that Islamic schools should have enough programs and activities to prepare their students to interact with the society at large in the best possible way. Parents should raise this point in their parent-teacher meetings and make sure that these programs are in place.

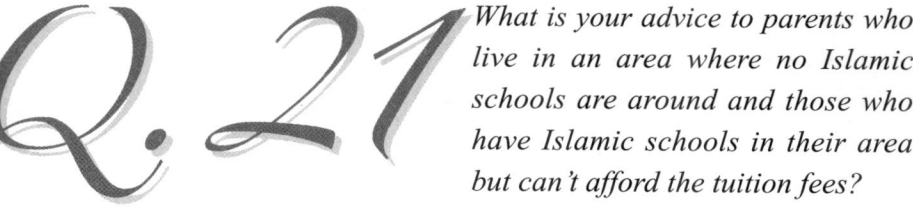

What is your advice to parents who live in an area where no Islamic schools are around and those who have Islamic schools in their area but can't afford the tuition fees?

Answer   There is no doubt that many Islamic schools across North America provide a much safer environment than many of the public schools, while at the same time trying their best to be at par with the public school system when it comes to academics. However, it is a fact that the number of Islamic schools in North America are very few compared to the number that would be needed to accommodate all Muslim children. In fact, these schools are only able to cater to the education of less than 5% of the Muslim student population on the continent. In addition, many Muslim parents who would love to have their children enrolled in Islamic schools may not have the financial means to do so.

Considering the above, does this mean that there are no other options for viable education in a safe environment for Muslim Children in North America? Far from it. There are definitely other options that can meet parents' needs for their children, but parents have to be involved in one form or the other. Here are some of the available options:

  • **Home Schooling:** Many Muslim parents have used this option. With the help of the Ministry or Board of Education in their state or province, they can obtain the curriculum, books, and other material required for their children's level and program, and then act as a teacher for their children at home to complete the program. There are many success stories of families who have home schooled their children, particularly those who made sure to provide platforms and opportunities for their kids to interact with other kids in society for the development of their social skills.

• **Public School System**: It is unfair to paint all public schools with the same brush. Some of them are safe, while others are not, and some of them do a wonderful job academically while others don't. As such, it is the duty of the Muslim parent to do their homework and find a good school in which to try to enroll their kids, even if it means moving to another part of town. In addition, parents need to be involved with the school in every possible way, such as the following:

- Consider being part of the parent-teacher committee or parent-teacher association of your child's school. It is a great opportunity for you to be in the inner circle and know almost everything happening in your child's school, as well as having first hand information that will put you in a much better position to suggest changes and modifications to certain practices and policies to accommodate the needs of Muslim children in the public school system.

- Volunteer for various school activities, such as helping in the school library, helping in your child's classroom, and providing resources and support to school organizers during field trips.

- Write notes to the school to announce Islamic events such as Ramadan and Eid.

- Participate with your children in the show and tell activities.

It is important to note here that while enrolling children in public school, parents shouldn't ignore Islamic education at home. The home will be the main source of Islamic education for children in public school, so parents have to be very dedicated and willing to do what it takes to ensure that their children have a solid Islamic understanding that will provide them with the support they need to be able to safely maneuver their way through the public school system. This could be achieved with the following:

• Providing a healthy, positive, loving, caring, and encouraging family atmosphere where children can freely express their views without fear of being snapped at or reprimanded.

• Being easily approachable and willing to dialogue and discuss any issue with our children in an objective and open manner. This approach will help our children's wellbeing and provide them with useful information to use when confronted with the same issues and questions by their peers.

• Being available when the child comes home from school to help him sort out his feelings and make sense out of what took place during his school day

• Living Islam at home and modeling good manners and behavior for our children.

• Teaching Islamic concepts and helping children to acquire good habits, such as saying the appropriate *du'a* for every occasion.

• Doing things together as family. Get the children involved in almost every family activity and make them part of whatever you do. Of course, take each child's age into consideration.

• Be fair and don't favor any child over the others. Try your best to treat them equally.

I'm of Middle Eastern origin and my wife is a North American who accepted Islam a few years ago. We have two daughters who are 11 and 13 years old. They have been very active in school and participated in Brownies programs when they were at that age. They made some friends who are not Muslim during their enrollment in Brownies. Recently they both asked us to go for a sleep over at the house of one of these friends. When I discussed the issue with my wife, I found that our views on this subject were 180 degrees apart, (completely opposite.) She sees nothing wrong with our daughters going for a sleep over at their non-Muslim friend's house, and I feel that this is not appropriate and that they shouldn't go. Can you please advise us on what we should do?

Answer   This is an important question that deserves a thorough answer. To start off, we'll give some general advice to both parents, and then, because it is not for us to decide if they should go to the sleep over or not, we will provide our view on the subject in the format of guidelines, with the hope that it will help all parents in general and the questioner in particular to make the right decision.

General advice

• Saying yes or no for a question like this should not be based on the cultural practices of the father or mother. If you base your answer on cultural practices, there will definitely be different views, and as the question indicated, father and mother will likely end up having completely opposite views regarding the matter.

• No matter what decision they arrive at, parents should provide a very clear explanation to their children. The explanation should be logical to the child, and should be given in a simple and convincing tone along with the feeling of love, respect and concern for the child. Failing to provide such an explanation may result in the children feeling that their parents are irrational. If parents themselves, at some point in the future, slept over at the house of a friend or relative, children may also feel that parents are applying a double standard.

Guidelines

• As children grow up, parents should establish the rules of their household clearly and communicate them to the children. Among those rules would be a rules related to sleepovers.

• The general rule with respect to sleepovers should be 'No sleepovers at others' houses'.

• The exception would be that if the family hosting the sleepover is known by the parents well enough to assess the potential danger to the child of a sleepover, and that following this assessment, the parents feel it is safe for her to go.

• Being proactive is highly recommended. Providing an alternative solution helps curb the children's cravings to ask for a sleepover. For example, parents can initiate a sleepover or arrange similar activities with Muslim children of close friends to compensate for the child.

• If the hosting family is trusted and the safety of girls in the hosting house is established, parents should also make sure that there are no boys in the house during the sleepover.

• The opposite is also recommended. If it is boys sleep over, the hosting house should have no girls during the sleepover.

• No girls sleepover should take place in a single parent house where there is no mother in the house.

As for the question, if the mom has done her homework and is sure of the safety of her girls because the above guidelines are fulfilled, then the girls may be allowed to go to the sleepover.

However, if the above guidelines are not fulfilled and there is a slight doubt as to the safety of the girls, the decision should be not to allow the girls to go to the sleepover.

Again in this case, we emphasize that parents should be very calm as they explain to the child why they made the decision they made. Speaking in a kind and soft manner will help the child to understand that his parents value him and take the matter of his safety very seriously. The child should not detect any irrational behavior from his parents and should not feel that either of them is angry with him. Also, if parents can propose an alternative to compensate for the child not going to the sleepover, this will be very good for his development and his long term relationship with his parents.

Q.23-A: I am planning to get married to a non-Muslim. We are currently engaged, and I am not sure if she will revert to Islam or not. I'm concerned about our future children. I've heard so many stories about Muslim men marrying non-Muslim ladies, and their children ended up going to church and not becoming Muslim. Is there anything that I can do now to avoid this future for my children insha'a Allah? Please give me some practical advice on how to deal with this. Thank you.

Q.23-B: My son is twenty-five years old. He is attracted to a non-Muslim woman that he works with, and is considering marrying her. I'm very concerned that if he goes through with the marriage, he will drift away from living an Islamic lifestyle and won't be able to provide a Muslim family environment for his children. What can I do to let him see that this decision is crucial and that he needs to be more careful about what to do?

Answer   These two questions are very important and deserve to be answered in great detail. As such, we will borrow our discussion from chapter three of our book "Blissful Marriage"[64] on the subject of "marrying from the people of the book."

"As indicated in *Surat Al Ma'edah*, Islam allows marriage from the people of the book, i.e., Jews and Christians. Allah says what can be translated into the following:

"This day are (all) things good and pure are made lawful unto you. The food of the People of the Book is lawful unto you and yours is lawful unto them. (Lawful unto you in marriage) are (not only) chaste women who are believers, but chaste women among the People of the Book, revealed before your time - when ye give them their due dowers, and desire chastity, not lewdness, nor secret intrigues if any one rejects faith, fruitless is his work, and in the Hereafter he will be in the ranks of those who have lost (all spiritual good)."[65]

It is important to note the following:

The Condition Stated in the Verse
This condition of "chaste women" stated in the above verse is nearly impossible to meet in today's North American society considering the following statistics:

---

[64] Drs Ekram & Mohamed Beshir, **Blissful Marriage** by amana publications, Beltsville MD, USA, second edition, 2007

[65] (Q 5, V 5)

- In the next 24 hours in the U.S. alone, 1439 teens will attempt suicide, 2795 teenage girls will become pregnant, 15 006 teens will use drugs for the first time, and 3506 teens will run away.

- One fourth of all adolescents contract a sexually transmitted disease before they graduate from high school.

The Practice of the Early Muslims

Although marriage to people of the book is allowed according to the previous verse, it was never recommended. As a matter of fact, most of the time, it was discouraged. The following incidents illustrate this fact:

- It was narrated that Jabir *RAA* said, "I witnessed the battle of Qadessiah with Sa'd, at which we married some of the women of the people of the book. When the battle finished and we returned, some of us divorced them and some stayed married to them."

- When Omar *RAA* learned that some Muslims were marrying from the women of the people of the book, he wrote the following to Hozaifah *RAA* in a letter, "It has reached me that you took a woman of the people of the book in marriage; I instruct you to divorce her."

Hozaifah answered him, "I will not do what you tell me until you tell me whether it is allowed or prohibited, and you explain the reasoning behind your instruction."

Omar's answer was, "No, I don't say it is prohibited, but I'm afraid that you may marry of the women who are not chaste" .

- In another narration, when Hozaifah *RAA* confronted Omar *RAA* saying, "Do you claim that this practice is prohibited so I should divorce her."

Omar *RAA* answered, "No, it is allowed, but those women are attractive and may spoil your relationship with your Muslim women."

Muslims in North America are a Minority

When discussing this verse, most Muslim scholars indicate that this marriage is allowed mainly in a society where Muslims are a majority. In this case, the general practices of the Muslim society may affect the woman from the people of the book and she may revert to Islam. Even if she doesn't accept Islam, the children are not in great danger of losing their Islamic identity because of the Islamic environment around them.

The Reality of the North American Condition

When we look at the reality over the past few decades in North America when Muslim men marry women from the people of the book, we find that the marriages often end in divorce. The children end up with their mothers because the court system often grants custody to mothers over fathers. In most cases, the children grow up as non-Muslims because of their mother's influence and their father's absence. We have witnessed these situations through our involvement in marriage counseling.

The Impact on Muslim Women

Another point that Muslims have to consider before making the decision of whether or not to marry from the people of the book is the impact that their decision will have on Muslim women. If many young Muslim men marry from the people of the book, while young Muslim women are not allowed to marry non-Muslim men, there will be an imbalance in the number of Muslim men and Muslim women at the marriageable age in North America. This will definitely put young Muslim women at a disadvantage. Some of these women may not find a husband and may even live the rest of their lives without marriage.

A Word of Caution
Considering all of the above reasons, our recommendation with respect to marriage from the people of the book is as follows:

1. At this point in time, this practice should be highly discouraged among Muslim men in North America.

2. In some extreme cases, it can be practiced provided that the following precautions are taken:
(a) The potential spouse must take medical tests to ensure that she does not have any diseases that may have critical effects on the family.
(b) The spouses must include an article in the marriage contract that indicates that, in the case of a divorce, the father will be granted custody of the children. If this is impossible, at least include an article ensuring that the children will follow the religion of their father, i.e. it will be their fathers' right to teach them Islam, and that their mother can't take them to church or any other religious institutions outside of Muslim institutions.

Now, it is important to clarify that, if the woman accepts Islam before marriage, the condition of being chaste should be disregarded, because when people take the *shahada*, Allah forgives all the mistakes and sins that they committed before they accepted Islam. The prophet *SAAW* said, "When a person accepts Islam, any bad deeds she previously committed are not held against her." [66]

For the reader in question 23 –a, we are glad that you are concerned about the future of your children and we hope that the above information has provided you with enough reasons to review your decision and pursue another way to find a spouse who will help you in protecting your future children and raising them as Muslims. As for the mother in question 23 – b, we believe that the above analysis will serve as a good basis for a serious and hopefully fruitful discussion between you and your son. Try to be very calm and composed during your dialogue with your son. Take your time and allow him to counter argue your points and repeat again the various points we indicated in our analysis. You may also seek the help of the Imam of your community or a prominent guest speaker during a visit to your community if you have this opportunity. If not, you may accompany your son to one of the national conferences or conventions that take place around the country and make an appointment with one of the guest speakers to talk with him. It may be costly but it is worth it. Please make lots of *du'aa* and we will do the same for you.

---

[66] Muslim

ROLE MODELLING

Q.24-A: If their father is smoking and doesn't pray, how will this affect my boys? I have 4 boys.

Q.24-B: What should I do if my husband doesn't get involved with parenting our children and leaves me to do all the teaching, and disciplining on my own? However, he still acts like he is the boss, though he does not get involved except to shout and yell at the kids when they do something wrong? what to do?

Answer   This is a very serious matter. Parents should lead by example. They should be their children's main role models. It is a well known fact among scholars of *Tarbiyah* that modeling is the most effective tool of parenting. This is absolutely true because it is a proven scientific fact that minds register pictures in a much more vivid way than words. When a child sees certain acts practiced by his parents repeatedly, he tends to imitate these acts more than if he is instructed to do these acts.

Allah *SWT* sent us Prophet Muhammad *SAAW* as our role model, telling us, "Certainly you have in the person of the messenger of Allah the best role model to follow for those whose hopes are in Allah and the Hereafter."[67] Parents should learn from the model of our beloved Prophet *SAAW* and model good behaviour for their children to follow. If the chil-

---

[67] (Q33 , V21)

dren's father is smoking and is not keeping up with his prayers, certainly they will be affected negatively by this behaviour.

Helping out with various family matters and duties is another recommended trait that the Prophet Muhammad *SAAW* has emphasized in his teachings. It was reported that "A'isha, *RAA*, was asked, 'In what way was the Prophet, *SAAW*, productive in his house?' She replied, 'He used to work for his family, meaning, he used to be in the service of his family. When the time for prayer came in, he would leave for prayer.'" [68]

In addition to the above, the family atmosphere is considered the most important factor that affects the formation of the personality of our children. As such, it is crucial for parents to provide a positive and healthy family atmosphere for the well-being of their children and their children's healthy personality formation.

Due to the above mentioned points, and since the consequences of the father's actions are very serious and will have a long lasting negative effect on the personalities of the children, it is very important that the father be advised to stop these irresponsible practices as soon as possible. This can be done in the following two ways:

> • Speak to your husband in a kind and gentle way about the negative influence of his actions on the children's healthy development. This conversation has to be done in private, and it's important for you to be very tactful in your approach. You

---

[68] Al Bukhari

should select an appropriate time for such a discussion (when he is not busy, tired, or distracted by something else), and at all costs avoid being confrontational and don't nag him. Your husband may not respond favorably to your request from the first session. As such, there may be a need to repeat the conversation more than once. It is important to observe objectivity, kindness, and gentleness during the discussion.

• You can also seek the help of one or more respected persons in the community to make your husband understand the seriousness of the matter and hopefully commit to changing his behaviour. Help may come via the gentle advice of the Imam of the mosque or one of the leaders or elderly respected members of the community. It is important to make sure that you seek the help from a person who doesn't have any personality conflicts with your husband and is respected by him. Your husband may be open to discuss the matter with certain individuals whose views and contributions to the community he values, but not with any one else. So try to find the right person for the conversation and seek his intervention in the matter.

We hope this will help you in solving this problem. Please try to make lots of *du'a* to Allah *SWT* to support you during this process and grant you patience and self control.

I'm a mother of three children, two teenagers and a toddler. When I was teenager myself, I use to rebel against the orders of my parents and I was even rude to them most of the time. I also used to be very short tempered.

When I got married and had a family of my own, I think I changed a lot, and I'm trying my best to raise my children the proper way and teach them to respect their parents and others. I feel that I'm not succeeding and I feel that my teens are doing the same things I was doing when I was their age. My question to you is, "Does our behavior as teenagers have an effect on our children's behavior? Will they behave the same way we behaved as teens, even if we changed our behavior when we become parents?"

Answer   As research indicates, and as we've alluded in many of our writings, there are many factors that affecting an individual's personality. The most crucial of those are family atmosphere, position within the family, genetic disposition, and methods of training.[69]

---

[69] For the details effect of each of these factors on the personality of human being, please refer to chapter one of our book ***Meeting the Challenge of Parenting in the West: An Islamic Perspective***, published by amana publications

Based on the above, we think if parents have changed their own behavior, and that whatever they were doing as teenagers is not part of their current behavior, their teens will not necessarily behave like them when they were teens. The behavior of your teen will mainly be the results of you and your husband's modeling, which covers the family atmosphere you are providing for them, as well as the methods of training you are using with them. The environment will without doubt also have an impact on your teen's behavior and attitude.

So, if you notice that your teen is behaving in a similar way to your behavior when you were teen, you are most likely still repeating the same behavior as a parent. You may think that you've changed, but it looks like you haven't really made a complete change, and that your teens are picking up certain elements of behavior from your model. In this case, we recommend that you go through the "Self Search process"[70] to make sure you recognize the sources of negative parental behavior you have as a parent and those of positive ones. The self search process will also help you to learn how to get rid of the negative parental behaviors you have and replace them with positive ones.

Of course, you also have to use the proper methods of training[71] as well as providing a healthy and supportive environment for the development of your teen.[72]

---

[70] See our book *Parenting Skills According to Qur'an and Sunnah* published by amana publications

[71] See chapter two of reference 69

[72] See chapter three of reference 69

Q.26

My husband doesn't pray regularly. He is very good in other areas of his life. For example, he is a nice person and takes good care of the family financially. We have three children. The oldest is 8 years. I'm trying to train him to be regular in his prayer, but he tells me 'dad is not doing his prayers. Why should I pray? If prayer is good, why is dad not praying?' What can I do to solve this problem?

Answer   The situation you described is very problematic. Modeling is extremely important, as children always look to their parents' behavior and model their own behavior accordingly. Any child in your son's position would have the same reaction. As such there is no simple solution for this problem. However, it looks like you have to work on two fronts, with your husband as well as with your son. We suggest that you do the following and hope it will help *insha'a* Allah:

1. With your husband

-Select a suitable time to discuss the issue with your husband. Start by talking about your children's future and what both of you want for them. Talk about the teen years and how difficult it is for Muslim kids growing up in this culture. Elaborate on the various risks and challenges facing them.[73] Talk about your worries and concerns that if both of you don't come up with a good plan to raise your children, they might be affected by the

---

[73] Please see details on this subject in our book ***Muslim Teens; Today's Worry: Tomorrow's Hope*** by amana publications chapter 1 and 2

negative elements of popular teen culture surrounding them. Explain how you believe that an Islamic upbringing is the only way to help your children stay safe while going through the adolescent stage. Emphasize the fact that you are worried that if you don't instill Islamic habits in them now, it will be difficult for them to resist all the temptations and avoid copying the promiscuous actions of their fellow teens.

- It is important that you and your husband have a common vision about the way you want to bring your children up, and that both of you work together on this vision. To achieve this, you must   be patient, wise and tactful. At any point in time if you feel that your husband is uncomfortable continuing the discussion, be ready to postpone it to another time. This is a major issue and will probably take several sittings.

 - From your side, even if your husband gets defensive, you should remain calm and courteous, rather than challenging, confronting, and blaming.

- After you reach a common vision with your husband on the above matters, mention to him what your son is saying and ask him how he wants you to respond to your son.

- We would like to warn you that more often than not, in situations like this, your husband may not respond positively to your concerns and may even get defensive. Don't get discouraged. Be patient because there is no quick fix, and rest assured that your husband is thinking about what you said to him. You have planted the seed and you need to carefully water it once in a while. As such, stay the course and continue gently to get the intended results *insha'a* Allah

2. **With your son**

• In addition to working with your husband to make him see the importance of prayer for the well being of your children, you should also emphasize to your son why we pray. Try to shift the focus from why your husband is not praying to why we as Muslims should pray and to the benefits of prayer in various areas of our life such as physical, spiritual, emotional, being in good company, etc.

• Mention to him how you will be pleased to see him regularly praying and trying to please Allah *SWT* .

• If he still asks why his father is not praying try to find an excuse for your husband. Mention that maybe when he was young, he was not lucky enough to find somebody to help train him to establish regular prayer.

• Mention that it is important for your son to help his father by making *du'a* to Allah *SWT* during his prayers, asking Him to help his father see the importance of *salah* and to start practicing it. The opportunity to make *du'a* is another important reason for us to be regular in our prayer.

• Emphasize to him the fact that Prophet Muhammad is our role model, and that if somebody is not performing all of their Islamic obligations, we should not take them as our example. Rather, we should always say look to the Prophet *SAAW* as our role model, and follow his example all the time. In the meantime, we should pray to Allah *SWT* to help the other person to also follow the example of Prophet Muhammad *SAAW*.

We believe that, if you work patiently on both fronts, the chances of a positive outcome with the help of Allah and regularly make *du'a* are very high *insha'a* Allah.

CONFLICT RESOLUTION

Q.27

I have two children. Ahmed is seven and Faheemah is four. In order to teach them sharing and train them not to be selfish, we make all their toys common toys that both of them have to share. They still fight frequently about toys and books. Once one of them holds it the other one wants it.

Answer   It is noble that you want to teach your children good qualities such as sharing and not being selfish, and we think parents should do their best to teach and instill in their children these wonderful attributes. You should be commended for doing this.

When it comes to toys, it is good to have some common toys in the house, as well as some toys that are designated for each child. Don't worry about frequent fights between the children. This is natural and your role as the parent is to teach them how to resolve these conflicts.

To solve the fighting problem between your children you should do the following:

• Set very clear rules of ownership. If the toy belongs to one child, he or she has the right to allow or not allow the other child to use it.

• If the toy is common (does not belong to a specific child) make sure that you apply an 'equal sharing' rule. Set a specific time, for example, 2-5 minutes, for each child to use the toy, then let the other child have a turn to play with it.

• When your children get into fights, don't rush to solve the problem for them. Allow them sometime to resolve the situation themselves.

• Deal with your children fairly. Don't favor one child over the other because of age. Consider the need of each to play with toys and enjoy their own toy.

At the same time as you are following the above suggestions, you can also do the following in order to strengthen the bond between your children:

• Observe fairness in all your actions with them

• Provide them with some games and toys that can only be played by more than one person. This will teach them cooperation and improve their social skills in dealing with each other.

• Tell them some stories about the importance of cooperating and how important it is to bond together. Make sure you do this by story-telling, not lecturing.

I have two sons, the older is six and the younger is two. Every time the two year old holds an old toy that belonged to his brother when he was a toddler, my older son rushes and grabs it from him, saying 'this is my toy.' How can I solve this problem?

Answer   This is natural behavior for older children if they were not coached to do otherwise. Usually, older children try to hold onto their toys even though they may have outgrown them. This particularly happens when they have a younger sibling who is trying to play with these old toys. As such, don't be alarmed by your older son's behavior. However, you should try to gradually change this habit. Here is what we suggest you do:

• Sit down with your older child and go through all his old toys. Let him pick one or two (or may be even a few) of them that are not necessarily age-specific or to which he may have a special attachment. Tell him that these are his toys and will always be his toys, and ask him to keep them in a special place so no one else will use them.

• Use this opportunity to allow him to play with some of the other toys. Since these other toys are age-specific, he will get bored very easily and realize that playing with them is not as fun as it use to be when he was younger. Talk to him about how fun it is to play with toys that are good for his age and let him know that it is better to let his younger brother use his old toys. Encourage him to give some of them to his younger brother as a gift and compensate him with something special when he does this.

• Whenever you buy a new toy for your older son, this presents a wonderful opportunity for you to let him give one of his old toys to his younger brother. Encourage him to teach his younger brother how to use the toy and praise him for his efforts.

Following the above tips will go a long way in helping your older son outgrow his attachment to his older toys. We would like to also indicate that this may take some time, and that your older son may not respond the way you would like from your first attempt. It may take a few trials, so don't give up. To help your older son during this process, we also recommend that you be very kind with him and don't express frustration or anger when he grabs the older toys from his younger brother. Try to be patient with him and use a gradual approach until you get the desired results *insha'a* Allah.

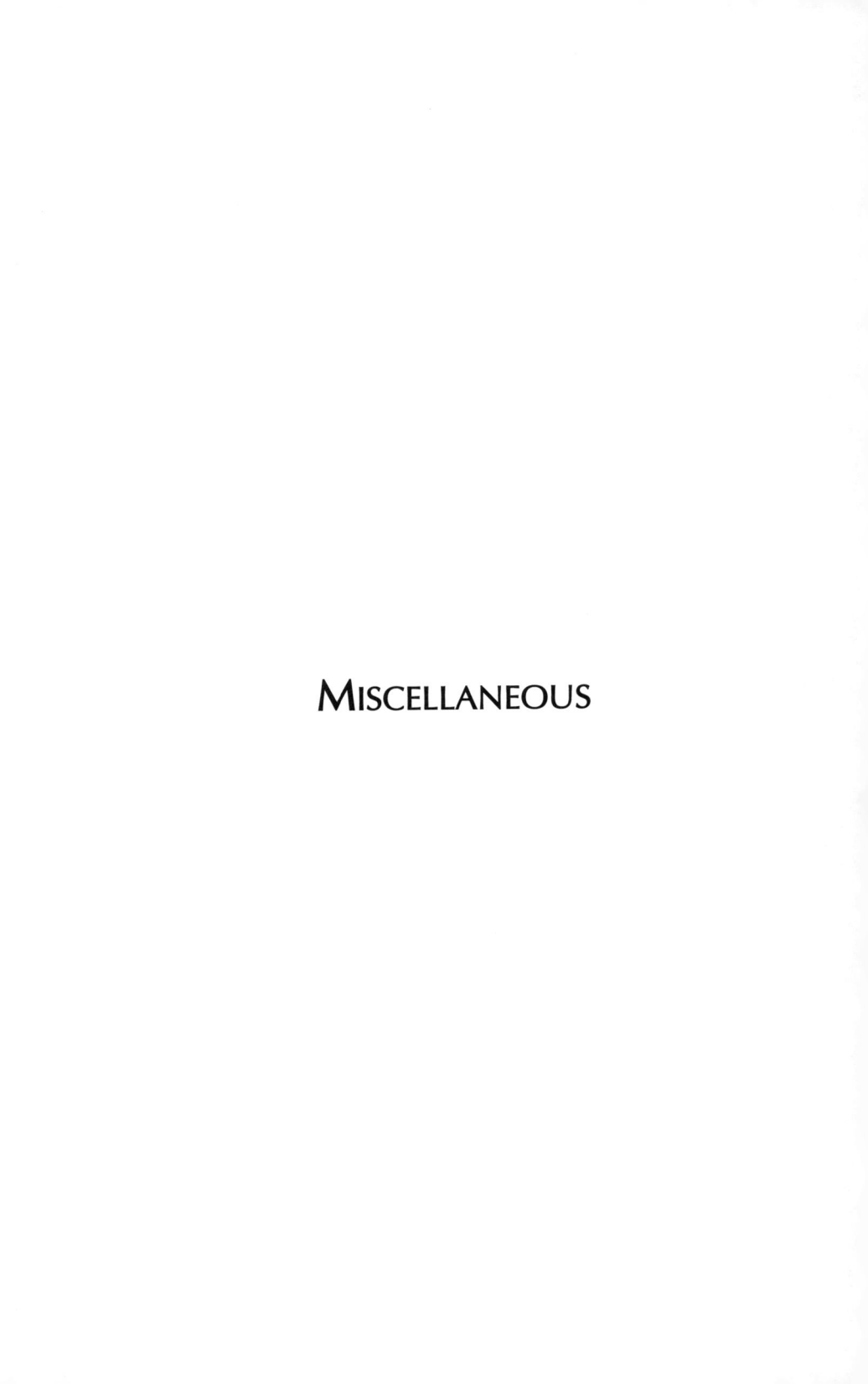

MISCELLANEOUS

Some parents put their children in a lot of extra curricular activities such as swimming, Arabic, Taekwondo, etc. So children are not left with any time to spend with family. Parents are driving most of the time. Please comment

Answer Islam is a religion of balance and moderation. It looks at the human being in a holistic way and tries to address all of his needs. It has teachings for healthy physical development as well as for positive spiritual, emotional, social, and intellectual development.

Muslim parents' responsibility is to raise a well rounded and justly balanced personality who doesn't go to one extreme or the other. As such, the education and training they provide their children should try to cover all of the above needs in a harmonized and integrated way. While regular and moderate sports activities will contribute positively to the healthy physical development of the child, excessive sports activities will leave the child exhausted and having no energy or time to positively develop other areas of her personality. These other areas are as important to the health of our children as the physical side of the personality. As such, parents should help the child to be organized and divide her time into several portions as follows:

• A portion for physical development which will include activities such as sports and gaining knowledge around good nutrition and proper diet

• A portion for spiritual development which will cover Qur'an memorization and understanding, learning *ahadeeth* of Prophet Muhammad *SAAW*, and making remembrance of Allah, etc.

• A portion for intellectual development which will be spent studying various subjects suitable to his age, and engaging in discussions with parents or older siblings to understand various facts of life

• A portion for social development to spend with her family (siblings and parents), her friends, and acquaintances to learn how to interact with others in a civilized manner

Not all of these portions have to be done at specific times of the day or on a rigid schedule; rather some flexibility can be applied. The key is that parents use each opportunity of their interactions with their child to develop their emotional, spiritual, intellectual, and social skills.

Parents also should use what it often thought of as 'lost time', such as when they are driving their children to activities or to visit their friends. This time, rather than being 'lost time' is a great chance to instill certain values and concepts in the mind and soul of your child. The prophet *SAAW* did exactly this when Ibn Abbas was riding behind him.[74]

---

[74] See the *Hadeeth* which was narrated in both Ahmad and At Termithy describing what the Prophet *SAAW* have advised Ibn Abbas when he was riding behind him

I'm a mother of three children ranging from 1 to 5 years old. I was very active in my Muslim community and I always volunteered my time and energy to help with various projects at the local level, as well as with national Islamic organizations. I believe that Muslims should be highly motivated, have superior zeal, and try their best to be in a state of alertness to serve their religion. I know that there are things that one can do to elevate the level of her zeal and I use to do it before having my children. Now with my three children and their limitless chores, I find it very difficult to keep my high motivation. Do you have any suggestions on what I can do in this situation to keep a lofty level of zeal, or is it impossible to do this with young children?

Answer   *Jazaky Allah Khayran* our dear sister for asking this very important question. Yes we agree with you that Muslims should try their best to have superior zeal and be part of the various projects taking place on a local level as well as at the national level. Of course the participation level is affected by the circumstances of the individual at the various stages of her life. We can't expect a mother of three children to contribute to these volunteer activities the same way as a person who is single and doesn't have many commitments toward others. However, it is very noble of you to think about this and try to keep a high level of enthusiasm and involvement in working for the sake of the *Deen* of Allah *SWT*. To help you with this noble cause we suggest a multi-faceted approach that covers various elements, to be applied at the individual level, the family level, and the Muslim Community level.

At the individual level we suggest the following:

• Remember that all deeds are judged based on the motives and intentions behind these deeds.[75] As such, proper intentions turn actions that are permissible (allowed matters and common chores) that we do daily into matters of *Ibadah* that we will be rewarded for *insha'a* Allah. So, at the beginning of your day, and before you start any chores for your children make sure you are focused and your primary motives and intentions (*Niyyah*) behind these acts is to please Allah *SWT* and carry out your duties as a Muslim mother who tries her best to raise strong confident Muslim children to carry the banner of Islam. With sincere intentions, you will be rewarded for every minute you spend with your children, and every minute you spend working for something on their behalf, and will not feel that your time is wasted, which in turn will help increase your motivation level.

• Realize and remember that for each time there is a *Ibadah* (worship) that is most appropriate. For example, when prayer time comes, the most important *Ibadah* is to perform that

---

[75] See the first *Hadeeth* of the **An-Nawawis Fourty Hadeeth** by Imam Al- Nawawy, translated by Ezzeddin Ibrahim and Denys Johnson-Davies, published by International Islamic Federation of Student organizations, 1997

specific obligatory prayer. Also at the month of Ramadan, the most important *Ibadah* is to observe fasting. For a student who has an exam the next day, the most appropriate *Ibadah* for him is to study for this exam, not to go to the mosque for a lecture or even to perform night prayer. Of course, this doesn't mean he should miss his obligatory prayers. He will have to perform them, but the rest of the time his focus should be to study for his exam. Also, for a mother of three children, in addition to performing her obligatory *Ibadat* (prayer, fasting in Ramadan, zakat, etc.), the most appropriate *Ibadah* for her is to spend enough time with those children, taking care of their needs (physical, educational, emotional, spiritual, etc.) and not necessarily to be very active with community projects at this stage of her life. As such, don't feel bad that you are spending more time with your children and not volunteering as much as you used to do with your community projects in the past. *Insha'a* Allah there will be many opportunities for you to be very active again with your community in the near future. Again, do it with the proper intentions so you will be rewarded for every minute you spend with your children.

• Taking care of children in the proper way could also be source of self development and motivation. Remember that one of the most important duties of parents, which is unfortunately neglected by many parents in North America, is to instill important Islamic concepts and values in the minds and hearts of your children. These values and concepts will help to develop justly balanced personalities with a high moral fiber and ethics to live by in this society. It will help to build the character of those children and provide them with strong conviction to resist societal temptations, particularly during their adolescent stage.

To be able to do this, parents have to do certain reading and learning of their own to understand these Islamic concepts properly, learn how to instill them in the hearts and souls of their children, as well as know how to answer certain questions about Islam to their children. All of the above will keep your motivation high and help you to learn new things about your *Deen insha'a* Allah.

At the family level, we suggest the following:

• We would like to remind fathers that according to most scholars, from an Islamic point of view, parenting is a shared and joint responsibility and duty between both parents (Mom and Dad). Both have to work together as a team and come up with their parenting plan, divide tasks, do their share and carry out duties in implementing their parenting plan. This doesn't mean that the father will spend the same amount of time with children as the mother, particularly if the father is working outside home 8-10 hrs a day and the mother is mainly working at home. The mother will continue to be the main care giver of the children. However, the father has to be part of the planning process and has to carry certain tasks related to the raising of the children. Another area where the father could help is to free the mother from taking care of the kids for one or two nights a week, so that she can attend a study circle to keep herself motivated or simply rejuvenate herself through any kind of appropriate entertainment with other Muslim sisters.

• Father and Mother should have a serious discussion about the family priorities. They should make up a priority list and keep the children at the top of this list. As a result of this process, the family may have to give up some of their old habits to be able to manage their time properly and save badly needed time for their children's development. For example, at this stage of their life, they may have to give up cooking fresh meals every day or even every second day. Mom and Dad could work together during the weekend to cook a few dishes, keep them in the fridge, and warm them on weeknights for dinner. Without a doubt, this will save much-needed family time to spend with the children and keep the motivation going. Eating leftovers or ordering food from a restaurant once in a while may also help. Every little bit will help in saving time and making sure we provide our children with the needed attention and care, as well as having time for our spiritual and mental development that will keep us motivated to work for the sake of this *Deen insha'a* Allah

At the community level, we suggest the following:

• Activities planned at the community level should always take family needs into consideration. Our communities consist of groups of families. Our families are not fathers alone, or mothers alone or children alone. Our families are a combination of all of the above (fathers, mothers, and children at various age groups). It is unfair to always organize activities for fathers alone and not include mothers and children. It is also unfair to organize activities for adults alone (mothers and fathers) and forget about children. Try your best to convince your community members and activity organizers to plan activities with families in mind. This means:

- Make sure that there is babysitting available for young children so mothers can attend the activity

- Make sure that there are interesting programs for pre-teens, and teens, alongside the main program for adults

- If this is not possible alternate activities so sisters can attend while brothers can take care of children and vice versa

We hope that the above will help you during this challenging time with three children. May Allah *SWT* keep us motivated and help us to carry out our duties to the best of our ability in various areas of our life.

Most of us were raised back home in the East where negative reinforcement was used a lot, but we still turned out to be good Muslims. So how come negative reinforcement worked out for most of us but it doesn't work for our children??

Answer

We don't really understand exactly what you mean by using negative reinforcement. Also, we don't clearly know what criteria you used to come to the conclusion that all of us turned out to be good Muslims. These are two important factors that, given more clarity, could help us give you a better answer to your question. However, these are not the only factors that affect the outcome of the parenting process. Environment, modeling, support systems, and the difference in the era you were raised are just a few to be named. As such, we could discuss and point out these factors in an effort to analyze your question. Here are some important points to consider:

- It looks like the comparison you are making between your generation and that of your children is rather unscientific. We think you are probably comparing them at two completely different stages of life, looking at your generation now at adulthood after settling down, achieving maturity, and awareness of their goals, while looking at the generation of your children at their adolescent stage. I'm sure if you scratch your memory a little and try to remember your own generation when they were teenagers, you will find many things that they did that are almost exactly the same as your children's generation now.

• For your generation, which was raised in majority-Muslim countries, even if negative reinforcement (whatever it means) was used with you by your parents, there are other factors in the lives of your generation that may have compensated for the inappropriate reinforcement, such as the following:

- The extended family provided huge support to the unit family and helped in raising the children. This kind of help is not available for the majority of parents here in North America. They have to do the parenting alone without extended family support.

- Your generation had built in support by living in a Muslim majority society. Growing up in a Muslim majority society provides tremendous support for parents who are trying to instill Islamic values into their children's hearts and souls. The majority's social behavior is nearly harmonious, homogenous, and accepted by the rest of the society. Also, Muslim behavior enhancers are plenty and constitute a great part of the support system for children. For example, there was always something related to Islam and its basic principles in various media sources (books, newspapers, radio, and television networks). *Qur'anic* recitation is always aired on radio and TV stations. The *Adhan* (call to prayer) can be heard regularly everywhere a child turns. Mosques are located in every corner of the city with scholars who are available to teach and answer questions almost 24 hours a day. Religious occasions are celebrated regularly. Parents are not shy to identify with Islam. On the whole, the atmosphere is very encouraging, conducive, peaceful, and supportive for anyone who chooses to adhere to Islamic values and practice them.

• Your children are not only deprived of the support system described above, but they are also faced with a completely different environment which presents them with many difficult challenges and tremendous sources of pressures, such as the following:

- Day-to-day peer pressure at school, including school dances, parties, dress problems for girls, friends, smoking and drugs, etc.

- Religious holiday celebration pressure, including Christmas and Easter

- Pressure in specific instances when Western Media report on incidents and events related to Islam and Muslims in a biased and unfair manner[76]

• The time factor is another important point to consider in this discussion. We are talking about two different generations, which means an almost 25 year difference. Many things have happened during this time that affect the environment of our children's generation, and the most relevant to this discussion are the following two factors:

---

[76] For detailed list of challenges and problems see chapter 3 of our book *Meeting the Challenge of Parenting in the West: An Islamic Perspective*

- New technologies, without a doubt, have contributed to the easy access to all kinds of information for our children's generation. Although some of this information can be beneficial to their academic advancement, it may not necessarily all be good for their social and spiritual well being. There are many problems related to Internet use and other electronic media to which our children's generation is subjected. Your generation was spared these problems, or, if you had to deal with them, it was on a very small scale.

- Moral norms have been majorly downgraded during the last few decades, and what was not acceptable morally in your generation is now the norm and is accepted by nearly every one from the children's generation. The moral bar has become very low and this trend is continuing.

I hope the above analysis has shed some light and provided you with an explanation for what you are looking for.

 *What would you say to parents who fight for power, meaning they always try to win their arguments and fights with their teens, and how can they instead become their friends?* We don't really understand exactly what you mean by using negative reinforcement. Also, we don't clearly know what criteria

Answer   The first thing I would say to them is, 'Fear Allah in the way you deal with your teens'. I hope this will open their minds and hearts to read the rest of the answer attentively and take my advice seriously *insha'a* Allah.

According to the majority of Muslim scholars, parenting is a shared and joint responsibility between mother and father. This means that they have to work together as a team to achieve the best results parenting their children. It starts with learning together the Islamic parenting skills as practiced by Prophet Muhammad *SAAW* and his followers, putting together a parenting (*Tarbiyah*) plan, and then dividing the plan into tasks to be assigned to both of them to execute.

In our Muslim communities living in the West, we have witnessed both extremes. In one extreme some fathers say to their spouses, "My job is to put food on the table and I have nothing to do with the children. Children are your responsibility." This is one extreme that is not acceptable by Islam. On the other end of the pendulum, some mothers spend their entire day talking with their friends on the phone, and when one of their children does something wrong, they tell them to stay in their room until the father comes home from work and deals with them. This is another extreme that is not also acceptable from the Islamic point of view. The first example is a father who is not participating in the parenting process at all, and leaving the whole job to be done by his wife. The second example is that of a mother who is neglecting one of her major duties. Both are wrong. Instead, both should work together as a team for the benefit of their children.

However, we should be clear that this doesn't mean that the father will spend exactly the same amount of time as the mother with the children, particularly if he's working long hours outside home, and the mother is mainly working inside the home. It means that the father is involved in the process and is part of the planning and execution of the *tarbiyah* plan with his wife. He is carrying out certain tasks to the best of his ability. Most importantly, it means that neither parent will undermine the authority or responsibility of the other parent, particularly in front of the children. For example, if one parent makes a certain decision related to one of the children, even if the other parent does not agree with the decision, s/he shouldn't interject on the spot in front of the child, expressing her/his disagreement with the decision. A better approach is to overlook the issue in front of the child, and then discuss it in private, as advised by the Prophet Muhammad *SAAW*. Then, after discussion, allow the other parent to modify the decision with the child. This approach will ensure that the child sees his parents working as a team without differences. Interjecting on the spot will send the wrong message to the child, who will feel that his parents are not in agreement on their parenting approach. As such, the child may abuse these differences between the parents to get his way.

To conclude this answer, we would like to emphasize that there is nothing wrong with trying to be close to our teens. As a matter of fact, it is recommended that we, as parents, should do everything possible to be close to our teens. Having a close relationship with them helps parents to be in touch with what is going with their teens and puts them in a better position to help with the many challenges they are facing. Here are some suggestions to help parents build a strong relationship with their teens:

• Understand their environment. You may be living under the same roof, but undoubtedly your teen's environment is very different from yours. Volunteering in your teen's school will give you a glimpse of her environment.[77] However, please be careful to pick the proper area of volunteerism in the school. It is not recommended to volunteer in your teen's classroom, or for activities particularly related to your teen. It is better to volunteer in a general area, such as the school library.

• Understand the changes that they are going through and what is taking place during the adolescent stage, and be sensitive to their feelings[78]

• Actively listen to them and allow them to express their thoughts openly without being judgmental

• Dialog with them as opposed to lecturing them. Encourage them to ask any questions they have on their minds without fear of being reprimanded

Both parents should be following this approach as part of their well-thought-out *tarbiyah* plan. No single parent should be competing against the other parent to win the teen's heart. The teen needs both parents and needs to feel that he is safe and secure in this relationship with either of them.

---

[77] See chapter one and two of our book **Muslim Teens, Today's Worry, Tomorrow's Hope,** published by amana publications

[78] Same as previous reference

 *How should parents greet each other in front of the children? Should it be a hug, a kiss, or only hand shakes? Are parents allowed to kiss on the lips in front of the children?*

Answer   The character of *Hayaa'* in Islam is a very important and core character, to the extent that the Prophet Muhammad *SAAW* said, "for every religion there is a core character, and the core character of Islam is *Hayaa.'*"[79] Prophet Muhammad *SAAW* also is reported to have said, "*hayaa'* is a branch of faith"[80]

There is no single word in the English language that is equivalent to the word *Hayaa'*, or can communicate the real meaning of the concept. The closest is a combination of modesty, decency, bashfulness, and the proper amount of shyness. Believing men and believing women are instructed to observe *hayaa'* in all their dealings. Protecting our chastity, covering our private parts, and dressing modestly are but a few items illustrating the observation of the concept of *hayaa'* in a Muslim's life. Seeking permission by all adults before entering a closed house or a closed room is highly emphasized and stressed in Qura'n. Even children who have not reached puberty yet are instructed and should be trained to seek permission before entering the closed rooms of their parents at specific times of the day. As soon as they reach puberty, they should seek permission all the time. Here is the translation of two verses from *Surat Al-Noor*.

---

[79] Ibn Majjah
[80] Al Bukhary

"O you who believe! Let your slaves, and those of you who have not come to puberty, ask leave of you at three times (before they come into your presence): Before the prayer of dawn, and when ye lay aside your raiment for the heat of noon, and after the prayer of night. These are three times of privacy for you. It is no sin for them or for you at other times, when some of you go round attendant upon others (if they come into your presence without leave). Thus Allah makes clear the revelations for you. Allah is Knower, Wise. And when the children among you come to puberty then let them ask leave even as those before them used to ask it. Thus Allah makes clear His revelations for you. Allah is Knower, Wise." [81]

The verses clearly explain why this permission should be thought at these times. They are times of privacy, when parents may be relaxed in the way they dress, or may be engaged intimately.

Based on the above verses and sayings of Prophet Muhammad *SAAW*, we feel that kisses on the lips or sexual hugs between parents are not right for children to see. However, showing affection is no problem as long as it is not done in an intimate way. It helps the children to feel secure and safe in the family relationship. A kiss on the check or the forehead or an innocent hug should be OK *insha'a* Allah.

---

[81] (Q24, V58,59)

I've heard this saying about training children and wasn't sure if it was correct or not? As the saying goes, training children consists of three stages. For the first seven years, treat your child like a king, for the next sever years (from 7-14), treat him like a slave and teach him what is right and what is wrong, and for the third seven years (from 14-21), treat him as an advisor. Is this a saying of the prophet PBUH?

Answer   The actual saying is "Play with your child for the first seven years; discipline him for the next seven years; and befriend him for the next seven years, then have no control whatsoever over him." There is a second saying that is almost the same with the exception of the last part, where it says: "then let him to have his own experiences."

This is not one of the sayings of the Prophet *SAAW*. Some scholars refer this saying to various companions of Prophet Muhammad *SAAW* such as Omar Ibn Al-Khattab *RAA*. Other scholars refer this saying to Sufian Al Thawrey *RAA*.

We would like to point out that, while the above sayings are words of wisdom, they should not be misunderstood. Many parents may use these sayings as an excuse not to discipline their children when they make mistakes as long as they are under 7 years old. As the questioner said, they are trying to treat them as kings. This is not what is meant by playing with your children during the first seven years of their life.

Rather, the saying means that at this young age, parents should play with them more often, as compared to the next stage of life, while still disciplining them whenever the situation requires disciplining. The practice of Prophet Muhammad *SAAW* is our reference and guide in everything. Although he used to regularly play with his grandsons Alhassan and Alhussain, on more than one occasion he *SAAW* disciplined and corrected their behaviour while they were in their first seven years of age. Here are a couple of these incidents:

> • "Ali *RAA* said, that The Prophet *SAAW* came to visit them and that while he was with Alhassan and Alhussain. Alhassan asked for water. The Prophet filled a cup and brought it to him. Alhussain jumped to take the water, but the Prophet prevented him. Fatima *RAA* said 'it looks like Alhassan is more beloved by you.' The Prophet said, 'no, but he requested the water first'"[82]

> • "Abu Laila *RAA* said that he was visiting the prophet *SAAW* who was carrying Alhassan, who urinated on the prophet's clothes. They rushed to take Alhassan from him, but the Prophet told them to leave him finish his business. He purified his clothes with water, then went to the *Saddaqa* house with the boy who took one date and put it in his mouth. The Prophet *SAAW* took it out and told him, 'we are not allowed to eat from the *Saddaqa*'"[83]

Another important point is that even though the second stage is characterized by discipline, this doesn't mean that parents should not play with their children during this second seven years of their life. It means that

---

[82] At-Tabarany
[83] Ahmad

the focus is on serious training, and that this is the age where all parents should start training their children to learn how to establish prayer and be regular and constantly practicing it, as we were advised by Prophet Muhammad *SAAW*.[84]

The Prophet *SAAW* taught and trained many of the young companions in important matters of *deen* while they were at this age, among them Anas *RAA* and Abdullah Ibn Abbas *RAA*. Here is one example of what he did:

"On the authority of Abdullah bin Abbas, who said: One day I was behind the prophet and he said to me:

'Young man, I shall teach you some words [of advice]: Be mindful of Allah, and Allah will protect you. Be mindful of Allah, and you will find Him in front of you. If you ask, ask of Allah; if you seek help, seek help of Allah. Know that if the Nation were to gather together to benefit you with anything, it would benefit you only with something that Allah had already prescribed for you, and that if they gathered together to harm you with anything, they would harm you only with something Allah had already prescribed for you. The pens have been lifted and the pages have dried.'"[85]

The third stage is characterized by treating our children as our companions. We should consult with them and give them responsibilities, but we can also still advise them and try our best to transfer our life experience to them.

Finally, we would like to emphasize that these stages are not rigid.

---

[84] Abu Dawoud and At-Termithy

[85] At-Termithy

They are only guidelines, and some children may need more play, or discipline, or befriending than others, even in the same age group. The maturity level varies from one child to another and also varies between different genders. Parents should be wise enough not to generalize and should deal with each situation based on knowledge and taking into consideration all relevant factors to ensure proper results and continue to be successful in their parenting quest.